T0276231

Daughter of History

Stanford Studies in Jewish History and Culture
Edited by David Biale and Sarah Abrevaya Stein

Daughter of History

Traces of an Immigrant Girlhood

Susan Rubin Suleiman

Stanford University Press

Stanford, California

Stanford University Press
Stanford, California

This book has been partially underwritten by the Susan Groag Bell Publication Fund in Women's History. For more information on the fund, please see www.sup.org/bellfund.

Printed in the United States of America on acid-free, archival-quality paper

Library of Congress Cataloging-in-Publication Data

Names: Suleiman, Susan Rubin, 1939– author.
Title: Daughter of history : a memoir / Susan Rubin Suleiman.
Other titles: Stanford studies in Jewish history and culture.
Description: Stanford, California : Stanford University Press, [2023] | Series: Stanford studies in Jewish history and culture
Identifiers: LCCN 2022034076 | ISBN 9781503634817 (cloth) | ISBN 9781503635616 (ebook)
Subjects: LCSH: Suleiman, Susan Rubin, 1939- | Jewish children in the Holocaust—Hungary—Biography. | Holocaust survivors—Hungary—Biography. | Holocaust survivors—United States—Biography. | Women college teachers—United States—Biography. | LCGFT: Autobiographies.
Classification: LCC DS135.H93 S85 2023 | DDC 940.53/18092 [B]—dc23/eng/20220726
LC record available at https://lccn.loc.gov/2022034076

Cover design: Daniel Benneworth-Gray
Cover photograph: The author at age 9, collection of the author.

To my family, the living and the dead

History with its capital H, its big axe . . .

—Georges Perec, *W or the Memory of Childhood*

These young people who spoke a foreign language and walked quickly ahead of you, eyes lowered, as if they were afraid of you, they were... Ah! they were foreigners... That word said it all. Floating people, without roots, emigrés, suspect.

—Irène Némirovsky, *The Dogs and the Wolves*

It's only by a habit borrowed from the insincere language of prefaces and dedications that a writer says "my reader." In reality, every reader is, while reading, the reader of himself. The writer's work is just a kind of optical instrument offered to the reader, allowing him to discern something in himself that he may not have seen without it.

—Marcel Proust, *In Search of Lost Time (Time Regained)*

Contents

Note on Pronouncing Hungarian Names

Although Hungarian appears as an impossibly difficult language to most non-natives, its phonetic system and spelling are simpler than those of English. That is because every letter or letter combination has only one sound, no matter where it appears in a word (compare to English b*ough*, th*ough*, th*ough*t, tr*ough*). Thus *zs* is always pronounced like the *j* in French *je* or the *s* in English *measure* (or the *zh* in Zhivago): Rózsi, Zsuzsi, Izsó. The letter *c* is pronounced like the English *ts*, as in Laci. The letter *s* or *ss* is always spoken like the English *sh* (Budapest, Kassa, Miklós, Pista), while *sz* is always like the English *s* in *sun* or *some* (Szeged, Kertész, Szabó). Here is a list of all the consonants or combinations that are different from English (with a sample name in parentheses), for quick reference:

c or *cz*: English *ts* (Laci, Koncz)
cs: English *tch* (Csaba)
g: hard, as in gas (Géza)
gy: like the *d-y* in *would ya* (Gyuri)
j: like the *y* in yellow (János)
ly: same as *j*, like *y* in yellow (Gergely)
ny: as in *Bunyan* (Manyi)

r: rolled, as in Italian (Rubin)

s or *ss*: English *sh* (Sándor)

sz: English *s* as in *sun* (Szabó)

zs: like *j* in French *je*, or English *s* in *measure* or *zh* in *Zhivago* (Zsazsa)

As for the vowels, their sounds vary according to presence or absence of accents:

a: like *u* in *mug* or *ou* in *young* (Magda)

á: English *ah* (János)

e: as in *bet* (Eszter)

é: like *ay* in *bay* (Béla)

i: as in *hit* (Iván)

í: like *ee* in *feet* or *beet* (Kína)

o: as in *or* (Konrád)

ó: as in *row* or *go* (Mózes)

ö: like the *u* in *burrow* or *burn* (Bözsi)

u: as in *oops* (Rubin)

ú: long, as in *hoop* or *loop* (Hús)

ü: as in French *tu* (Fülöp)

Now see if you can pronounce *Zsuzsi* (*zhu-zhi*) or *Jancsi* (*yun-tchi*) without even thinking about it!

Prologue
The Silver Pin

She had pinned it on the collar of her black dress for the formal photo: a silver flower long and slender, the sculpted leaves spreading on both sides of the stylized petals, with two symmetrically placed pearls in the middle. Today, it has little or no commercial value; the pearls are slightly yellowed, and if one looks closely one sees many imperfections on their surface. But back then, in Budapest, whenever I saw my mother wearing it, I thought of it as a precious thing. My father gave it to her shortly before the photo session, a sign of prosperity and survival. And of love, too—for despite their being profoundly mismatched, as I came to think later, a passionate bond existed between them. They had married for love, against his father's wishes, had survived the war with their only child, and soon they would be seeking a new life, far away from the world they knew. Even in my adolescent rages against them, I had to admit they did not lack courage or pluck.

That last photo session in Budapest took place in the spring of 1949, a few months before we left Hungary. Mother had curled my hair for the occasion, in long corkscrew curls that hung down to my shoulders, and she too had been to the hairdresser. I can imagine her thinking, *Capture this moment before we turn our back on it.* I was nine years old. Five years earlier, we had been hiding from the Nazis in a house in Buda, with false papers, false names. But that too was behind us now.

Nessa, my five-year-old grand-daughter, has been exploring the wooden box on top of my dresser in which I keep earrings and a few odd pieces of jewelry. When she finds the silver pin, she turns to me: "Why don't you ever wear this, Immy? It's pretty." Pins are for dressing up, I tell her, and in these days of the corona (as she calls it), we don't dress up much. But suddenly I have an idea. "Here is a little test for you." A test? Her eyes sparkle—she loves challenges. Pin in hand, we stand in front of the family photos I have hung in the hallway. "Look carefully at the picture of me and my parents. Do you see this pin anywhere?" The picture shows the three of us, Lilly and Miklós seated close to each other and me between them. It's high up on the wall; Nessa needs a stepping stool. She climbs on it, looks up, straining to see. "Your mom was wearing it!" she exclaims triumphantly.

Strangely, I don't remember her ever wearing the pin after we came to America. Was this modest relic of postwar Budapest unworthy in her eyes? Or was it associated with a country and a city she had no desire to remember? She had lost most of her extended family in 1944, deported to Auschwitz with the help of the Hungarian government. She never spoke about those uncles and aunts and cousins, and I had never met them—they were in the provinces, far from the capital; but in 1993, while I was living for a few months in Budapest, I made a pilgrimage to the city in northeastern Hungary where my mother was born and where some of the family had lived. She spent her summer vacations there as a child; I can't even begin to imagine what it felt like for her to learn, at war's end, that all those people were dead.

Some immigrants retain their ties to the old country. I have known Hungarian Jews who still referred to Budapest as home, decades after they had just barely escaped being shot into the Danube by Hungarian Nazis—that was quite the sport in the fall of 1944. Some survivors left the country soon after the war, like us; others waited until 1956, fleeing when the borders became temporarily crossable after the failed revolution. They all started going back for visits in the 1960s and 1970s, when "goulash communism" made life in Hungary quite pleasant again, especially for Hungarians with American passports and dollars. My uncle Laci, Mother's brother, returned to Budapest every summer for more than thirty years, right up to his death. Communism or no, the Gerbeaud pastry shop on Vörösmarty Square still served the best sour cherry strudel, and you could dine outdoors on chicken paprikas with *nockerli* at the Duna Corso restaurant on the bank of the Danube late into the night. Not to mention music and theater, the best in the world, he assured me whenever I saw him.

My mother had no truck with such nostalgia. She never went back to Budapest, and she reminisced about her youth in that great European capital only if I pushed her hard. "The Gellért baths, I went there often when I was courting," or "The Fish-

erman's Bastion on Castle Hill has beautiful views of the city."
Generally, she sought advancement and novelty, not memories.
She had a talent for small talk with strangers, and within a few
weeks after we arrived in New York, she had established several
outposts of acquaintances in the neighborhood. She frequented
the children's clothing shop on 86th Street near York Avenue,
where she would chat with the owners in a mixture of German,
Hungarian, and broken English as she looked for outfits for
my baby sister. She did not hesitate to ask them for a discount,
given our status as new immigrants. I often felt embarrassed
when I went with her, especially when she pushed me forward
to translate for her or when she started telling people she had
just met about her most intimate concerns: her worries about
money, her anxiety about our future, her doubts about my hair!
("You must do something about your hair" would become the
refrain of my teenage years.)

It occurs to me that maybe she did wear the pin in America, and it is I who have blocked it from memory. During my
adolescence I was desperate to be American, just like everyone
else, unmarked by signs of difference. Did the pin, which I had
found splendid in Budapest, become a reminder of our foreignness? I had adored my mother back there, so beautiful and lively,
always willing to play one more game of numbers (what's six
times four, what's five plus eight, what's thirty minus seven?)
or read me one more story. But I was often ashamed of her in
America, the immigrant mother who never learned to speak
English properly and whose insistent voice, with its deep vowels
in the back of the throat, never adapted to measured tones.

Now I feel ashamed, with a different kind of shame, when
I think about how little I valued her as an adult. But there is
anger there too. If I gradually became incapable of feeling love
for her—or of expressing love, which in a sense is the same
thing—was it not her fault as well as mine? She loved me, I

knew, and admired my successes; although she didn't read my books, she was proud that I had written them. But she was tactless, I tell myself, she didn't know how to listen, was interested only in material things. "Rich or poor, it's good to have money," she would often say with a laugh, repeating a joke she had heard somewhere—as if to excuse herself, or to admonish me.

Yet others loved her. After almost twenty years of widowhood in Miami Beach, she married again and her new husband doted on her. He was a retired dentist, Hungarian-Romanian, a widower; they got along well together, a real couple. When she became ill a few years later, he took care of her, and when she died a few years after that, aged almost eighty, he mourned her as if they had been together a lifetime. After her death, I kept hearing from people who had known her—she had been the belle of Lincoln Road, one old lady told me. She was fun to be with, she had a thousand friends.

My sister and I often talk about her now. She could be impossible, we say, but she was brave and energetic and had lived through a lot.

We inherited her photographs and her few pieces of jewelry. The silver pin came to me, along with a delicate gold orchid pin she had acquired in America. I put that one in my jewelry box; the silver pin disappeared into a jumble of old trinkets in a drawer. Devalued, like my mother in America? Yes, but not discarded. Waiting.

A few years ago, I dug out the pin from the drawer and, after vigorous rubbing with silver polish, managed to get it to shine. I even pinned it on a black jacket before heading out to teach. The gold orchid, when I wear it, reminds me of my mother, but it is simply a pretty object, carrying no strong emotion. The silver pin evokes bruises and ambivalence, emotional knots difficult to untangle. I only wore it once.

Proust's narrator, in that most famous passage of the novel where he dips a madeleine into a cup of tea, discovers that the taste revives a whole past world and time, intact. The immense edifice of *In Search of Lost Time* emerges from that single moment of revelation, what he calls involuntary memory— but of course that's an artistic conceit, not how things really happened. In real life, Proust spent several years and embarked on false starts before arriving at the structure of the novel, and he kept adding to it up to the day he died. He compared his book to a cathedral—immense, but not quite finished. What really matters in the search for lost time, we discover, is the process itself, and the result will be not a perfect whole but a life in pieces. No writer before Proust had shown as he did the kaleidoscopic nature of time and reality, where everything seen depends on who is looking, from which standpoint, and when. The Narrator's first inkling of this occurs when he is still a child, during a carriage ride when the church steeples around Combray keep shifting with every curve in the road. Similarly for people: Odette, the woman Swann pursues with jealous frenzy for several years, becomes, once he has married her, simply a woman he once loved and who was not even his "type."

In 2019, in that far-off time before COVID, I moved to the Washington, D.C., area to be near my younger son and his family, after retiring from more than three decades of teaching at Harvard University. Six months later, I, who was often in a plane to somewhere, found myself, like so many others, forced to stay put. My imposed stillness propelled me toward my relics. For religious true believers, relics are sacred remains associated with a saint or deity. My relics are ordinary objects, but they carry an emotional charge: the silver pin, old black-and-white photographs, the miniature chess set my father bought before we left Hungary. Some are not even material but exist only in my memory: a fraternity pin I wore for a few months in college, a recording of Heifetz playing the Beethoven violin concerto.

I cannot expect my relics to help me achieve wholeness, but I can aspire to reconciliation. In accounting, reconciliation is the process of ensuring that two sets of records are in agreement; in human relations, reconciliation is the process of mending a broken relationship. In my history, the records are often missing and the gaps and blanks can only be filled by imagination, or else must be left open. Is it possible to mend a broken relationship with a person who is no longer there to participate in the process? Can one mend a broken relationship to time and space, to home? How many cities have I called home? No straight lines but zigzags, breaks, departures, returns.

What is the opposite of broken? Intact. Unbroken.

Unbreaking: the process by which the broken is mended, with the cracks still showing.

Part I

Budapest

1

Postcard to Zircz

St. Valentine's Day, 1944. Lilly Rubin, a Jewish woman living in Budapest, sends a picture of her four-year old daughter to her sister Magda, who is hiding somewhere in France. A month later, the German army will invade Hungary and Adolf Eichmann will set up his headquarters in the capital; the roundup and deportation of provincial Jews will be accomplished with amazing efficiency, eliminating all of Lilly's extended family. But she doesn't know that now. Does she know about the Warsaw ghetto, about Treblinka, about the deportations from France? Does the name *Auschwitz* mean anything to her? I dream about this as I finger the photograph, then flip it to read the inscription on the back, written in her spidery handwriting: "To my sweet good Magduska, with much love and many kisses from little Zsuzsika." My aunt Magda, Mother's younger sister, had emigrated with her husband and daughter to France in the 1930s. Evidently, this picture was enclosed in a letter: to Magduska from Zsuzsika, the diminutives showing intimacy and familiarity, though in fact she had never seen me. Beneath the message, the date: *Budapest, 14-2-1944.*

I have fished the photo out of a drawer where it lay along

with others, helter-skelter, still in the original plastic bags and manila envelopes where Mother had kept them. Some of the black-and-white photos are torn, stained, of people whose names I no longer know, if I ever did. Some were clearly torn from an album, with bits of black paper stuck to the back. She had carried them around since August 1949, when we escaped from Hungary. I can imagine her on that summer day: she has to pack a suitcase, not too big, not too heavy—we are about to set out on foot across the border. What do you take with you on such an occasion? A few pieces of jewelry (there was not much anyway), warm clothing (it's August, but one never knows), and of course photos. But the album is too heavy, the pictures will have to go solo. "Just a few, when she was a baby, then a bit older, then from last year when we had the photographer come to the house—she wore the new dress I had had made for her." She hurriedly tears out the photos and stuffs them into the suitcase.

They're mixed in with colored snapshots I had sent her over the years: me with my two boys, me and my husband before our divorce, and earlier, before our marriage. Among the black-and-white photos is one of me at my college graduation, standing next to my mother, smiling, looking lost. Like a fatherless child? My father had died of a heart attack the previous summer, just before the start of senior year. But looking lost, feeling lost, had been familiar to me since childhood.

I had seen most of the old pictures while Mother was still alive, on the rare occasions when she consented to talk about our life in Budapest, the life we had left when I was ten years old. Usually, she avoided the subject: "That's behind us, forget about that," she would say firmly—but she said it in Hungarian, a fact that undercut the meaning of her words. The past is another country, historians have said. Can you forget a country whose language you still speak? My mother and I always spoke Hungarian when we were together.

I visited her in Miami Beach once or twice a year, and she would bring out the photos if I begged her, naming the people who were unfamiliar to me: provincial uncles and their families who had perished in the Holocaust; two of her cousins who survived, beautiful young women who had given her photos inscribed in the back with *Love to Lilly*. We would also look at pictures of me as a baby, a toddler, a schoolgirl. ("That was when I was a boy," I would joke at the photo of me at six months, lying on my stomach, almost completely bald.) "How cute you were, see, so blond!" she would say, fingering a picture of me at age two. Or: "I always liked that blue dress on you—we had it made in 1948, the year Granny left." And then, at last, she would start reminiscing: "Do you remember our Sunday hikes in Buda, our trips to the bookstore on Andrássy Avenue? You loved those books about Zsuzsika, the little girl who had your name—when you finished one, we'd go and buy the next one in the series. And the ice skating rink in City Park, where I would watch you skate." Yes, I remembered. I always shivered from the cold at the skating rink and didn't enjoy it, but she wanted me to learn how to skate and take ballet lessons and play the piano, all the things she had missed out on in her childhood. I was her only child (my sister was born much later), while she had grown up with three brothers and a sister in a family that had become fatherless when she was still a teenager. She had had no time for luxuries, and she wanted me to have them.

The photo she sent to her sister in 1944 was posed in a photographer's studio. Mother had made a special appointment with the fancy photographer, and the session probably lasted for several hours. In the end, she chose two pictures. In this one, my hair is loose around my shoulders, with a big silk bow on top; I wear a pretty cotton dress and a gold chain around my neck; a straw shopping basket hangs from my left arm, while the right hand holds the leash of a toy poodle on wheels. I am a young lady going out to do her daily shopping with her dog. Facing the camera, I smile and my eyes sparkle. Imprinted on the bottom right-hand corner is the name of the studio: Mosoly Albuma, Album of Smiles, with its address and phone number. At least some people were still smiling in Budapest in February 1944.

The other photo from that studio is even more absurd. With my hair in braids and two small bows instead of the big silk one, an apron over my pretty dress, I stand in front of a toy stove, my right hand resting on the lid of a pot sitting on the stove: busy housewife. Once again I'm smiling at the camera, this time even more broadly— I must have been aware of the silliness of the pose.

Mother loved beautiful things: the silk bows, the gold necklace. Maybe she didn't want to know what was happening. Maybe she thought we were safe. Hungary was Germany's ally, though by then a reluctant one. The Germans invaded in March 1944 to make sure it didn't bolt, and to take care, at last, of the Hungarian Jews.

About forced labor, at least, she knew: the photo with the toy stove is addressed as a postcard to her brother

Izsó Stern, at a postbox number and the number of a regiment. The Hungarian army had begun conscripting Jewish men into forced-labor service in 1940, and my uncles Laci and Izsó were among them. I have read about the forced-labor units, seen a few films too. At first, the men were relatively well treated, if one can say that about civilians forced to work long hours clearing woods and carrying rocks, undernourished and ill-clothed. Later, it got much worse. In the winter of 1943, the Hungarian army was routed by the advancing Russians in Ukraine, at the river Don; Jewish conscripts, now seriously deprived of clothes and shoes and food, were set to clearing minefields ahead of the regular troops. If they were not blown up, they starved or froze to death by the thousands, or died of exhaustion, or were beaten or shot for sport.

My father too spent time in forced labor, but Mother always said he had been released after a few weeks, thanks to her entreaties to the authorities: he was a rabbi, he worked for the Orthodox Community Bureau, he had a young child to support, she had pleaded. Somewhat to my amusement, my aunt Rózsi, my father's younger sister, told the same story, but according to her it was she who had pleaded and obtained his release! The main thing was, he had returned safe and sound not long after being taken. But a document I discovered only recently, which my father filled out in 1945, after the war was over, states that he had been in forced labor from December 1942 to February 1944—more than a few weeks. The document also states—in his careful handwriting, which I recognize instantly—that he had been in Russia, the worst possible place to be in forced labor. If the dates are correct (I say if, because he may have had reasons to prolong his captivity on paper—documents are not always one hundred percent trustworthy), he had returned from captivity on February 9, 1944, five days before my mother sent the photo of me to her sister. But she must have taken me to the photographer before that, which strikes me as an odd thing to do at the time. I suppose life went on, even if your husband was in a forced-labor unit in Russia (if indeed he was there).

My uncle Izsó died in forced labor—that we were sure of, although we never knew exactly where, or when. His brother Laci, who was in a different unit, had lost track of him early on. For a long time after he returned, Laci kept repeating, whenever Izsó's name was mentioned: "He was too gentle, he didn't know how to scramble for food, allowed others to take advantage of him—if only I had been there to help!" Laci always landed on his two feet, or so he thought. Personally, I think his survival owed more to luck than to any cleverness on his part. But these things are complicated. Maybe there was cleverness as well.

Now here is this postcard featuring me as a four-year old housewife, addressed to Izsó, in a regiment in a place called Zircz. My mother's message to him reads: *With much love to my dear uncle,* signed with my name, Zsuzsika. No date. There is a stamp with a postmark, indicating it was actually sent, but the postmark is illegible, even with a magnifying glass. Assuming that she sent this photo around the same time as the one to her sister, the card must have gone out in mid-February 1944. Was he dead by then? I hope not. I hope he received the card and smiled at his little niece's absurd pose. He was very fond of me, everybody said. I hope the photo made him smile.

But he did die, if not then, later. How did the picture get back to my mother? Perhaps it was returned, *Addressee deceased*? But there is no return address on the card. Or maybe it came back with a package of my uncle's effects after his death? No, that would have been too civilized—and besides, there was never any official notification of his death. Maybe, when he saw that

he was dying, he gave the photo to someone along with other papers and asked him to return it to the family if he survived. I imagine the scene: 1945, summer or early autumn, my grandmother is still waiting for her son. A man knocks on the door, stands in the doorway, looking uncomfortable, shifting from foot to foot: "I brought you this, Izsó asked me to." No, that's melodrama. I don't know how the photo got back to us. Maybe he was given a leave from his unit in 1944 and brought it home with him, before he returned to die.

I look for more signs. The card is addressed to Stern Izsó, Hungarian style, last name first. After his name, the letters *k.m.sz.* In Hungarian, forced labor is called, euphemistically, labor service, *munkaszolgálat*; *m.sz.* is obviously an abbreviation for that, but what does *k.* stand for? This is the time to consult my bible on these matters, Randolph Braham's big book on the Holocaust in Hungary. Braham gives two words beginning with *K* that went with *munkaszolgálat*: *közérdekű*, "public," and *különleges*, "special." Public labor service in the army, special labor service in Ukraine. It was special all right, unarmed, with no uniform, checking out minefields.

Where is Zircz? Sounds foreign, not Hungarian. Ukraine, the eastern front? I need a detailed map, which today is easy to find. Zircz (or Zirc, that's what the map says) is the site of an ancient Cistercian abbey in northwestern Hungary near the Austrian border, not far from the city of Veszprém. Veszprém has been renowned as a center of learning since the days of Hungary's first Catholic king, St. Stephen, who reigned in the eleventh century. Zircz is not in Ukraine but in authentic, historic Hungary, Magyarország—it was just one of those ironies to put a forced-labor camp in such a town, I tell myself. But then, Dachau is proud of its medieval churches, and Buchenwald was a stone's throw from Weimar, where Goethe had lived and worked. Culture and barbarism, close cousins.

At least it wasn't the eastern front. When my mother sent him that picture of me in front of the toy stove, Izsó –if he was still alive, and still in Zircz—was not checking out minefields, merely suffering from cold, hunger, backbreaking labor, the brutality of guards.

I fish out another photo, a small portrait of Izsó. He was a gentle man, with an oval face, brown eyes, wearing small, black, owlish glasses that look oddly fashionable today. His brown hair, smoothly combed, sits high up on his forehead; he is starting to get bald. He wears a dark gray suit, white shirt with soft collar, and wide striped tie; he is smiling slightly, with closed lips. A gentle man.

On the back of this photo, there is some very faint writing for which I need the magnifying glass. *Stern Izsó*, then his address in Budapest (which was also our address and my grandmother's; we all lived in one large apartment) and a date and place: *1904 Nagymihály*, evidently his year of birth and birthplace, then a more precise date, March 22, no doubt his birthday. Beneath

that, his mother's maiden name, *Lebovits Teréz*, then an official stamp with a notation in black ink and an illegible signature. The notation consists of a number, like an ID number, below which is a word that could be *láttam*, "I've seen him," followed by a date: *1942, 12/30*, and the signature. On December 30, 1942, an official person saw him, or gave him permission to leave, or to return. He was thirty-eight years old. The official stamped the back of his photo, and it too eventually found its way back to my grandmother and from her to my mother.

On page 338 of Braham's book, I find the following information: in November 1942, the Ministry of Defense required all Jewish men aged 18 to 48 to register. "Each affected Jew had to bring along two snapshots, one of which, after it was stamped by both the recruitment center and the local bureau for vital statistics, was to serve as a 'registration certificate.'" What I hold in my hand now is Izsó's registration certificate, stamped and dated and bearing an official signature. Braham reproduces a similar photo, front and back, and I see that it carries the same vital statistics as Izsó's: date and place of birth, permanent address, mother's maiden name. It too has a stamp and a signature; its date is December 22, 1942, eight days before Izsó's. Evidently, people were following the ministry's orders. The unidentified man in the book (it was Braham himself) was born in 1922; he was much younger than my uncle. But Izsó wasn't old. Thirty-eight is not old, when you lead a normal life.

Hungary has many place names beginning with *Nagy*: Nagyyaranypuszta, "great golden plain"; Nagyerdő, "great forest"; Nagylengyel, "great Pole"; Nagyszentjános, "great Saint John." Nagymihály, Izsó's birthplace, is "great Michael," named after the archangel. In 1904, it was a busy industrial town in north-eastern Hungary near the Carpathian mountains, part of the Austro-Hungarian Dual Monarchy, aka the Habsburg Empire. World War I put an end to the monarchy and rearranged the map of Central Europe, distributing many border regions to other countries. Today, Nagymihály is in far eastern Slovakia and is called Michalovce, the county seat of its region. In 1910, 32 percent of the population was Jewish, just slightly less than the Catholics (39 percent). As far as I can tell, there are no Jews living there today.

The Stern family all came from that part of the world: Izsó's parents, my grandparents, were married and lived for a while in Ungvár, today Uzhgorod in Ukraine, less than twenty miles east of Michalovce. In 1944, Ungvár had an even larger Jewish population than Nagymihály; many trainloads of Jews were sent to their death from Ungvár.

Izsó was my grandparents' first child, born before they moved to Budapest, but like his siblings, he was a child of the capital, at home with its pleasures. I rummage for more pictures of him. Here are two small snapshots, clearly from before 1944.

In one, Izsó stands with bare chest among a group of smiling men and women, all wearing bathing suits. Maybe it's a Sunday morning at the swimming pool on Margaret Island, or at the Gellért baths. Izsó leans forward, his elbows resting on the back of a wicker armchair in which a young man is reclining; Izsó's shoulder touches that of a blond woman who is sitting on the arm of the same chair. At the bottom of the picture, two little girls lean against the legs of the man and woman behind them, probably their parents. I have no idea who these people are; only Izsó's face is familiar. (Odd, that I should recognize him instantly on the photo when I have no memory at all of the living man.) He is wearing his owlish black glasses. His hair is slightly tousled; his expression, though serious, is relaxed. He never married, but he evidently had good friends. He looks happy.

In the second picture, he wears his dark gray suit, with a white shirt and tie as in the registration photo. He sits on a park bench with a young couple dressed in summer white. The woman's dress has a polka dot pattern, and she wears a fashionable straw hat with flowers and a ribbon; the hat is at an angle, low over one eye, giving her a coquettish look. She is smiling. The man's hat is a light gray fedora, almost incongruous with his white suit. They sit very close to each other, and she wears a diamond ring on her left hand. Maybe they have recently gotten engaged. Despite their well-dressed appearance, there is something provincial about the way they look. Izsó is bareheaded, sitting at a slight distance from them. They may be provincial cousins from the large Stern family, on a visit to the capital—the three of them have been walking around City Park and have sat down for a rest. Or maybe the scene is not in Budapest, and it's Izsó who has gone to visit them in their hometown. Wherever it is, it's an occasion worthy of a photo, of celebration on a sunny summer day.

Provincial Jews from Hungary were almost all deported, close to half a million. Very few came back. Like Izsó, this couple will soon be dead, but they don't know it. I feel offended by the obviousness of the tragic irony, the scalding but too-easy sense of time's irreversibility these images produce. The people are long gone, while I am here, and I know what happened to them. But please, no philosophizing. Look at the way she leans against her lover's arm, the way she wears her hat, at an angle, like Marlene Dietrich. The way the shadows play over her neck and face, over her smile. Just look.

The last picture I find of Izsó is a postcard-size photograph of a group of men, like a class picture: one row sitting, three rows standing, tallest in back. Behind them is a large open door, to a hangar or barrack. The photo has a long crack down the middle, mended with transparent tape on the back. Someone had torn it in half, then changed their mind; or maybe it was folded to fit in a pocket and got torn that way. The men are dressed in winter clothes, jackets and sweaters and overcoats. They wear no uniforms but look regimented. Most of them appear to be wear-

ing a tricolor armband on their left arm (some of their arms are hidden)—no doubt the colors of the Hungarian flag: red, white, and green. Most are bareheaded; a few wear wool work caps. One man, chubby, wears an army cap—he sits to one side and wears a white cook's apron over his wool jacket, a dishcloth slung over his shoulder. My uncle Izsó stands in the back row at the extreme left, bareheaded, in a dark overcoat, with a light-colored scarf around his neck. He is unsmiling, looking straight at the camera. They are all unsmiling, except the cook and one other man squatting in the front row. Why is that man smiling? He is one of the conscripts, wearing an armband. It must be the camera—some people can't help smiling whenever a camera appears. But it's not a happy smile; he is in half profile, glancing sideways at the camera.

Nothing is written on the back of the card, nor does any label or marking appear on the photo itself. Yet there is no mistaking it, this is a group of Jewish forced laborers: their pose, their look, their armbands all indicate what they are. I count twenty-nine of them, plus the cook; since he has no armband, he may belong to the regular army.

The men all look in relatively good health; the picture

must have been taken in the early days, maybe right after Izsó registered in December 1942. Or maybe even earlier: many Jews were called up in '40 or '41, allowed to return home after a few months, then called up again. But why the class picture, and how did it reach my mother? Bizarre idea, a souvenir photo of a forced-labor camp. Was this in Zircz, or did Zircz come only later, when no more photos were taken?

Were there similar pictures, now lost, of the surviving brother Laci? Did he too receive a photo of me in his labor camp, busy at my stove or holding my toy dog by the leash? Was she also planning to send a photo to my father, not knowing he was about to arrive home? I don't know, and there is no one around anymore to ask. My father died decades before my mother, and my aunt Magda and uncle Laci are gone too. While they were alive, we never talked about these things, and it appears I never turned the pictures over to see what was written on the back. The only people who mourned Izsó after the war were my grandmother and his siblings, who needed no photos to remember him.

I put the pictures back in the drawer without trying to sort them. Someday I'll do it, get a nice album, organize them neatly, write notes about them for my children. Meanwhile, I ask myself: was she thoughtless and frivolous, taking me to the photographer like that, in February 1944? Of course she could not know what would happen a few weeks later: all her provincial cousins and uncles and aunts rounded up and murdered, we ourselves in hiding, hunted. But still, how could she continue her bourgeois rituals—the appointment with the photographer, the satin bows and silly poses—so late into the war? Unless it was that very perseverance that showed courage and insight: she would continue to affirm her life, our life, even in the face of destruction.

2

Yellow-Star House

In the middle of the night, my mother wakes me up and dresses me. She and my father and grandmother speak in whispers, hurrying. After I'm dressed, still half asleep, my mother takes me by the hand and runs down the stairs with me. Or maybe she picks me up and runs, carrying me. She has torn the yellow star off her jacket. At the bottom of the stairs, we slow down. There are gendarmes on both sides of the street door, the concierge standing next to them—a plump youngish woman, dressed in a heavy coat and felt slippers. Her job is to identify the Jewish tenants so that none leave the building on their own. She sees us but says nothing.

Mother and I walk past the concierge and the soldiers, out into the street where day is dawning. She holds my hand tightly. We walk up the street toward the yellow church, keeping a steady pace. *Don't look as if you don't belong here.* After we turn the corner, we start to run. A mad, panicked dash to the next corner, then a stop, out of breath. Saved.

We lived in an apartment building in a busy part of the city, on the Pest side. Three balconies stood out on its façade, forming an upside-down triangle. Ours was one of the two on top, and from between its wrought-iron railings you could see people walking in the street below. The first thing you saw when you entered the building and crossed the vestibule was the large cobblestoned courtyard, bordered on each floor by a gallery with wrought-iron railings; if you looked up, you had the feeling of being in an intricate cage. To the left was the wide stone staircase, leading to our apartment on the top floor, three flights up. I would run up and down the gallery outside our door, and whenever I stopped and looked down into the courtyard, I felt dizzy. I held on to the railing, my heart pounding with excitement and fear, knowing all the while that I was safe. Then my grandmother would call me in for a snack of buttered bread, thickly sliced rye with a heavy crust, topped by a piece of salted green pepper. ("Oh gross!" my children grimace when I tell them about it many years later—but they love green pepper, it must be in the blood.)

Our street was called Akácfa utca, Acacia Street. There were no acacias there, or any other trees; not far away was Kis Diófa utca, Little Walnut Tree Street, which was similarly devoid of vegetation. But we were close to Andrássy Avenue, a wide boulevard with plenty of trees, which stretched all the way to Heroes Square and City Park. Outings on Andrássy Avenue were always a treat, with its elegant shop windows, the imposing opera house, and most importantly the pastry shops where we would stop and buy ice cream cones in warm weather, or cones of chestnut purée topped with whipped cream in winter on the way home. On the corner of our street stood a yellow church; a few streets away in the other direction were the Orthodox synagogue and the Orthodox Community Bureau, where my father worked.

Despite the church on the corner, it was mainly a Jewish neighborhood inhabited by observant Jews, many of them quite poor. (The richer, more assimilated Jews lived in another part of Pest, closer to the Danube, or across the river in Buda.) On Friday mornings, you would see women lining up at the covered market near our house to buy carp for the evening meal—they boiled it and served it cold, in its jelly, before the chicken soup and the boiled beef. For the Sabbath meal the next day, my grandmother would often make cholent, the bean and beef stew that would bake all night at the baker and be carried home after the morning service by the Christian maid, who also turned the lights on or off in our apartment. According to the Law, Jews were forbidden to work on the Sabbath, and that included even the lights.

On March 19, 1944, German troops invaded Hungary, upending the lives of Jews from one day to the next. Not that life had been all that easy before. Men were conscripted into forced labor, like my father and my uncles. And before that, before I was born, Admiral Horthy's government had started passing "racial protection" laws (protecting the "real" Magyars from the Jews, that is), creating a gradual stranglehold on Jews in business, in academia, in the liberal professions. But until the Germans marched in, Jewish women and children did not have to fear for their lives; and while forced labor killed many thousands of men, the killing was not systematic, just a by-product of the cold, of insufficient food and sleep, of being worked to death.

The Germans came because Hitler knew that Horthy, technically an ally of Germany, was beginning to eye an exit. D-Day was not far off, and it didn't take much wisdom to realize that Germany was losing the war. Invasion, for Hitler, was a way to keep Horthy in his place—and most importantly, it was a way to take care of the last big piece of unfinished business in the "solution of the Jewish question." Hungary had more than six hundred thousand Jews living within its borders, and Adolf

Eichmann was sent to Budapest to make sure they did not re
main there. Within ten days of the invasion, all Jews above the
age of six had to wear a yellow star on their lapels, on pain of se-
vere punishment. Within a month, the Jews in the northeastern
part of the country, where my mother's extended family lived,
were herded into ghettos by Hungarian gendarmes; without the
cooperation of the Hungarian government, the deportations
would have been impossible. The first transports to Auschwitz
left on May 15; by the first week of July, almost all of the provincial Jews, around four hundred fifty thousand people, had
been rounded up and deported. At that point, Horthy stopped
the deportations.

The Jews who remained were almost all in Budapest, and
the fact that they were not systematically deported explains why
Hungary today has the largest Jewish population in Eastern
Europe. (The Jews of Budapest suffered only—"only"—from
random deportations and murders, such as the shooting of more
than twenty thousand into the Danube by Hungarian Nazis, the
Arrow Cross, in the late fall of 1944.) In June 1944, the government designated close to two thousand apartment houses all over
the city as yellow-star houses (or just starred houses, since everyone knew what that meant), and forced Jewish residents from
other buildings to move into them, assigning a whole family to
one room. The house where I lived, 59 Acacia Street, became
one such house. Attached to the wall above the number on its
entrance door, a large yellow star informed the world that Jews
lived there. A few Christians lived there as well—I remember
a lady on our floor who told me stories about baby Jesus, and
whom I liked because she was very pretty. People who already
lived in the house could stay there—the Jewish tenants simply
had to make room for the newcomers. At least we didn't have
to move.

I learned about this history many years later, after I began to un-forget Hungary—that is how I thought of the awakening that came upon me around the time my mother entered her last illness, a few years before her death. Until then, the ten years I had spent in Budapest, the first ten years of my life, were a distant memory to which I felt almost no connection. Of course I knew what had happened to me in my childhood, but I never talked about it, never told stories about that time to my husband or my sons. I barely even thought about it myself, too busy with my career, with motherhood, with all the obligations of a working American woman's life. I was a working American woman, having put much time and effort into becoming one. Eventually I even achieved a notable success, becoming one of the few tenured women professors at Harvard before I turned forty-five. This too cost a great deal of effort, as well as a divorce—nothing in life is free, as my mother always said.

What I call my un-forgetting was the gradual process of allowing memories to surface and wanting to write about them. The process began when, seeing my mother ill, I decided to return to Budapest and take my two sons with me. Michael was fourteen, a gangly teenager; his brother Daniel was seven. I realized, although I did not formulate it exactly that way at the time, that I wanted to show them the city where I had been a child and where their grandmother, my mother, whom they thought of as old and sick, had been a young woman. Once the idea had taken hold, the travel plans followed. Budapest was still behind the Iron Curtain, but traveling there had become quite easy by the 1980s. We took a plane from Paris to Budapest in August 1984, exactly thirty-five years after I had left it with my parents.

I did not know exactly what I expected from this brief vacation in "Mom's city," as my sons called it; but its consequences turned out to be enormous, for after that trip I started writing about my childhood— just a few fragments at first—and my teaching and research took a major turn toward history. Until then, people in the academic world knew me as a literary theorist because my first book had been heavily influenced by the then new and intellectually exciting structuralist theories from France; some thought of me as a feminist critic, for I had published several essays on issues of women and gender and would soon publish two books on the subject. The turn toward history was yet another zigzag, as I call these changes in intellectual direction.

Some scholars specialize in one thing, burrowing deeper and deeper and becoming the recognized expert on the subject; others tend to prefer breadth to depth, and that is true of me—even as I am working on one thing, I am already eyeing another. But there has to be a trigger for such moves, some personal involvement or passion. The trigger for structuralism was my desire to master a new, challenging method of studying literature, which had the added prestige and glamor of being French. The trigger for feminist criticism came from the thrill of reading Freud seriously for the first time, and finding that he spoke to me. He harbored some very Victorian ideas about women, but his attention to the inner life was enormously appealing after the aridity of structuralism, and his emphasis on sexuality and the body appeared as a necessary starting point to many feminists of my generation.

Returning to Budapest in 1984 proved to be the trigger for my turn toward history—not only personal history, which was already present in my and others' feminist work (we often said, jokingly, that feminist criticism had finally allowed us to say *I* when writing about literature), but also the collective kind, History with its capital *H* and big axe, as the writer Georges Perec punned on the word *hache* in French. Teaching and writing about World War II and the Holocaust, including the way that time was remembered by those who had been children then, became a major preoccupation of mine over the years that followed. I became a scholar of war and memory.

All this because, after years devoted to forgetting, I had suddenly wanted to see Budapest again. A decision made upon impulse can sometimes determine a whole life.

The first memories that surfaced, as my sons and I walked around the neighborhood where I had lived in Budapest, were of the spring and summer of 1944, when the Nazis came. I have often thought since then about the night when Mother and I walked past the concierge and the soldiers at the entrance door, and have asked myself why the concierge let us go. Was she moved by the sight of the mother and child, or had my parents paid her off? Probably it was both—people's motives are often mixed. But the financial motive seems likely, for my father succeeded in skipping out a little while later. My grandmother stayed behind and was eventually taken to the ghetto (the Budapest ghetto was created quite late, at the end of November 1944), where she lived until the war was over. In first grade after the war, when I told this story to my classmates (we all had a story, recounted with melodramatic flourishes on the way home from school), I found it miraculous that she was not taken to Auschwitz, or lined up and shot into the Danube like the people another girl told about. Many people in the ghetto had died of illness or starvation, but Granny had survived. It was at that time, I believe, that I began to conceive of history as a form of luck.

The next scene takes place on a farm far from Budapest. My parents had decided to leave me with the Christian farmers for my safety. Mother probably explained this to me, although I have no recollection of it now. Nor do I remember actually arriving at the farm. I remember being there, scared.

The kitchen of the farmhouse has an earthen floor, a long wooden table in the middle; in one corner stands a massive butter churn. I am standing next to the table with Mother and the farmer's wife. Mother has dressed me in a frilly dress and white leather shoes, like the ones I wear in the city. She kisses me and says it won't be for long. Then she leaves. I cry.

Now I am running across the large dust-covered yard, chased by geese. They are immense, honking furiously, wings aflutter. They're on my heels, stretching their necks to bite me. I run into the kitchen, screaming. The farmer's children laugh and call me a city girl. I can't stop crying and feel as if I will burn up with shame. As the tears stream down and smear my face, I make a promise to myself: they will not see me cry again.

How long did I stay on the farm? I don't know. It felt like a long time. It was summer; I must have turned five while I was there. Meanwhile, back in Budapest, my father managed to get false papers for all three of us. He and my mother decided to take me back, danger or no. But by the time she came for me, I was used to the farm. I am crouching in the dust with the other children, dressed only in a pair of panties, barefooted, busy playing with some broken bits of pottery. I see my mother but don't go to her. I hardly look up when she runs to me and hugs me.

Many years later, when I first saw a therapist because I was feeling hopelessly depressed, unable to make any decisions about my life, he jumped when I told him this memory. I had never attached much importance to it, but he insisted. It took me a long time, and more therapy, to acknowledge that first separation as a crucial episode of my childhood, one that put into place an emotional mechanism I would often rely on later: when confronted with a devastating loss, grit your teeth and move on.

When I first started to remember these scenes, I was convinced that running from the house and running from the geese on the farm occurred in that order: first we escape, then I am sent to the farm, after which we are reunited. But as I read more detailed accounts of the summer of 1944, I realized that my memory had misled me, placing the two scenes in a logical and chronological order they did not necessarily have. History often proves to be more complicated, and more difficult to fit into a single coherent narrative, than memory makes it out to be.

What I learned is that after their forced move to the yellow-star houses at the end of June 1944, Jews in Budapest remained in danger, since the Nazis and the most rabid antisemites in Horthy's government hoped to deport them all. But by the end of August, the situation had improved. Horthy had decided not to cooperate in any more deportations and to seek a separate peace with the Allies. It's possible that my parents sent me to the farm in July, when they feared the worst, but took me back at the end of the summer and we escaped from the house later, when the situation became dangerous again. Unfortunately, I never thought of asking my mother about this while she was alive; she might not have been able to answer in any case, for she was notoriously vague about everything that concerned our life during those days. She told me once, for example, that she had a nose operation around that time to make her look "less Jewish," but she could not recall (or would not say) exactly when the operation took place. It may have been in 1944 but could also have been earlier, as soon as Hungary entered the war on the side of Germany in 1941.

On October 15, 1944, Horthy took the final step and announced on the radio that the Third Reich had lost the war (by then, Paris had been liberated for almost two months) and he was ordering all Hungarian military personnel to lay down their arms. The general rejoicing among Jews after this announcement lasted less than a day, for the Hungarian Arrow Cross leader Ferenc Szálasi, backed by the Germans, reversed Horthy's order that very evening and took over the government. (The Arrow Cross was a party modeled on the Nazis, like the National Socialist Party in Romania.) On the 16th, Horthy and his family went into exile in Germany; on the 17th, Eichmann returned to Budapest (he had left in July, when the deportations stopped) to help the Hungarian Nazis deal with the remaining Jews. On November 29, the Budapest ghetto was officially established, and its boundaries included our house on Acacia Street. My grandmother didn't remain in our house, however, but was transferred deeper into the ghetto to a center for old and sick people living alone—it was there that, miraculously, she survived the siege, until the Soviet army liberated the ghetto in the middle of January.

One curious fact stands out, which I found in Randolph Braham's authoritative history of the Holocaust in Hungary: "On October 16, the Yellow Star houses of Budapest were sealed off for about ten days. Jews were not permitted to leave their own buildings whatever the emergency." Braham provides no details, but that fact alone would be enough to explain the feeling of panic and the role of the concierge standing by the door, so strong in my memory. According to this revised version of the memory, then, the running from geese took place in the summer, after which I rejoined my family on Acacia Street; then in October, when the Arrow Cross's reign of terror began, we skipped out of the house and went into hiding with false papers. (Before she died, my father's sister, my aunt Rózsi, confirmed that we had left the house in October.)

I have never found out how we obtained the false papers, which appear to have belonged to real people named Jakab, refugees from Transylvania. *Jakab* looks like *Jacob*, but oddly enough it's not a Jewish name in Hungary. I suppose my father obtained the papers through people he knew at the Orthodox Community Bureau, where some young Jews had started a resistance group specializing in false documents. At any rate, thanks to our papers, my parents found a job as caretakers on an estate in Buda. The owner of the estate was an old noblewoman, a sculptress. I have no visual memory of her, but I imagine her as a tall, thin, kindly lady with white hair—like the Old Lady in the story of Babar, which I read a few years later. According to my mother, the old lady became very fond of me, even invited my mother to give me an occasional bath in her bathtub. On most days, Mother washed me while I stood in a small enameled basin on the floor next to the stove in our room. The room was so small that I would bump into the stove and burn myself if I wasn't careful. We had to make fires in the stove by then; it was autumn, turning cold.

My name is Mary. Mother whispers to me every morning not to forget it, never to say my real name, no matter who asks. I tell her not to worry, I won't tell. I feel grown-up and superior, carrying a secret like that.

Besides the old lady and us, four other people lived in the house: the lady's young nephew, recently married, with his wife, and an older couple who were also caretakers of some kind. They had been with the lady for many years and were suspicious of us. One day they asked me what my mother's maiden name was. I said I didn't know, and told my mother. She told them not to ask me questions like that: Couldn't they see I was just a baby? Her maiden name was Stern, a Jewish name. I knew that name; it was my grandmother's. Luckily for us, I didn't know what *maiden name* meant.

When winter came, more people arrived, relatives of the old lady. We all lived in one wing of the house to save heat. During the day, the warmest place was the kitchen or a glass-enclosed veranda that received a great deal of sun. The lady's nephew and his wife spent all day on the veranda in wicker armchairs, reading or playing cards. I liked to watch them. The young man especially had a languid, almost petulant air that fascinated me. I recall him as tall and handsome. My mother said he was an "aristocrat," which I understood from her intonation to mean something like "beautiful but weak." Watching him turn the pages of a book or run his fingers through his long wavy hair, I felt totally infatuated with him; at the same time, perhaps because of my mother's intonation as she said the word *aristocrat*, his gracefulness filled me with a kind of scorn.

For Christmas, we decorate a tree. I sing "O Holy Night" and receive presents: my mother taught me the song during the whole month of December. A Christ-child lies in a cradle beneath the tree. I am fascinated by the lifelike figure of the holy baby and by his mother's golden hair, but most of all I love the shining colored globes and the streams of glittering silver on the tree. Sometimes I feel sorry that we're not really Christians—we could have a tree like that every year.

In January, it turned bitter cold and snow fell. There were air raids at night, and we all started sleeping on cots in the basement. It soon became clear that my father was the man of the house. He made sure that we all gathered in the basement during air raids, even during the day. He listened to the shortwave radio and told us when the Germans began retreating. When the pipes froze and we had no water, he organized our nocturnal expeditions to gather snow.

How can I describe those winter nights? For years they remained in my memory as an emblem of the war, of the immense adventure that, with hindsight and retelling, the war became for me. A dozen shadows covered by white sheets flit across a snow-covered landscape. The sheets prevent us from being seen from the air, blended with the white ground and trees. Mounds of soft snow, darkness and silence—and with all that hushed beauty, a tingling sense of conspiracy. We carry pots and pans, scooping the cleanest snow into them with a spoon. When a pot is full, we take it inside, empty it into a kettle on the stove, then go back out to gather more. Three kettlefuls, my father says, will give us enough water for two days.

I don't know how many times we gathered snow, in fact. Maybe only twice, or once. No matter. I see myself, triumphant, smug, impatient for the boiled snow to cool so that I can drink it. As I bring the glass to my lips, I meet my father's eyes. We exchange a look of pleasure. I am five years old and I am drinking snow. Outside, bombs are falling. Here in the steamy kitchen, nothing can hurt me.

The Russians arrived in February. But first, we had German guests. A detachment in retreat invaded the house and set up radio equipment in our kitchen. They were distant, polite, ordinary. I had imagined monsters, like Hitler. (Hitler had horns, he was a giant.) My mother prepared meals for them, listening to their talk—they had no idea that she understood them. She would report their conversations to my father, but there was nothing new. Defeated or not, to us they were still a menace. After a few days, they left. I felt extremely pleased with us, clever Davids outwitting Goliath.

A few nights later, a bomb fell in our backyard. It made a terrific noise, and for a moment we thought it was the end. But when it turned out to have missed the house, we became quite jovial. As soon as there was enough daylight, we trooped out to inspect it. Whose bomb it is, we do not know; but there it sits, less than a hundred feet from the house, in the middle of a crater it made in landing, round and dark green like a watermelon. Somehow it all seems like a joke, even though we keep repeating how lucky we are, how tragically ironic and ironically tragic it would have been to get killed when the war is almost over.

The Russians arrive huge and smiling, wrapped in large coats with fur on their heads. They are our liberators; we welcome them. When they see my father's gold watch, they laugh delightedly and ask him for it. We don't understand their words, but their gestures are clear; my father takes off the watch and gives it to them. Then they ask my mother to go to their camp and cook for them. They put their arms around her, laughing. She points to me, laughing back and shaking her head: Who will take care of the little girl? They insist, but she holds fast. I feel frightened. Finally, they let her go.

After that, everything becomes a blur. How much longer did we stay in the house? Did we ever tell the old lady who we were? She was sick, according to my mother, and died during the last days of the war. But I have no memory of that.

In 1945, sometime between March and May, we walked back to our house, crossing the Danube on a makeshift bridge. All the real bridges had been bombed by the retreating Germans. Walking between my parents, holding each one's hand, I felt madly lucky and absolutely victorious, as if our survival had been wholly our doing and at the same time due entirely to chance. I was not aware of the paradox then, or if I was aware of it, could not have expressed it. But as I grow old, it occurs to me that I have often felt that way about my life: seeing it, for better or worse, as my own creation, and at the same time, contradictorily, as the product of pure luck.

That day, I mostly stared and tried to register everything—

storing it for future use, though I knew not exactly what. A dead horse is lying on its side in the street, its legs stretched out; someone has cut a square hole in its flank for meat. From time to time, a bombed-out wall shows where a house had been. We pass empty stores, their doors wide open—looted, says my mother. Inside one, on the floor in front of the counter, a white-haired woman lies dead. I cannot take my eyes from her, despite Mother pulling me away. Who killed her? Did they do it for money? What does her skin feel like, now that she is dead—is it cold and leathery? After a while, I stop thinking and even looking. I concentrate on putting one foot in front of the other.

On our street, all the houses are intact. We walk into ours, through the door where the concierge stood the year before. The courtyard is covered with debris, and there are holes that look like bullet holes in the walls; otherwise, everything appears the same. Up the stairs to the third landing: the lock on our apartment door is broken. Inside, the windows are all shattered and dust lies over everything, stirred occasionally by a breeze. The sky through the glassless window frames looks so near you can almost touch it.

I am no longer Mary, but for a moment I cannot remember my name.

3

Light Blue Wool Dress

In the fall, we ordered a dress from Madame Orbán, the children's dressmaker. It was 1948, the war was definitely behind us, and the Communist Party crackdown was only a glimmer on the horizon. Budapest ladies still had their dresses made in a salon for important occasions, and even their daughters' if they could afford it. There were specialized dressmakers for children, where you went and picked out a model from among the books of colored drawings in the waiting room and then went again for several fittings, just like the grown-ups. The model I chose was made of pale blue wool, falling in soft folds to a few inches above the knee. The sleeves were short and puffy, with tucks all around. But what really drew the eye was the large front flap in the shape of a V, from the shoulders to the waist, edged with a white hand-sewn ribbon made up of tiny white flowers. Inside the V were more white flowers, slightly larger than those on the edge, and in the center a much bigger one that could also have been a snowflake. On one side of the dress, at hip level, a small half-moon pocket was outlined in the same white flower-ribbon. A lot of hunched-over hours and eyestrain went into the making of that dress.

We were flush that year, for Mother's business was going well. She had opened a kosher butcher shop with a man who knew about meat—she took care of the cash register. Her earnings, added to my father's salary at the Orthodox Community Bureau, allowed for luxuries. That was the year of the grand piano, of ballet lessons at the opera school, of the Viennese lady who took me for walks and gave me French lessons. And of the light blue wool dress.

Mother had a photographer come to the house to take pictures of me in the new dress; she planned to send them to my grandmother, who had left for America a few months earlier. She braided my hair with special care that day, tying each braid with a white silk ribbon and leaving a few inches of unbraided hair to float freely at the ends. On top she rolled the hair into a sausage shape, as if it were on a large curler, held up by bobby pins. The Hungarian name of this confection, *tarék*, refers to a rooster's crown. I have never seen it anywhere else, but it was popular among elementary school girls in Budapest after the war.

I find it hard to distinguish, now, the part of this that belongs to memory and the part that comes from simply staring at the photos. They are black and white, yet I remember well the pale blue color of the dress. But I have no actual memory of wearing it or seeing those white flowers from the inside, with my eyes as they were then, not today's eyes, scrutinizing, weighing. And the little girl in the photos, Zsuzsanna, only child of Miklós and Lilly Rubin, Zsuzsika as she was called by those who loved her? She was I and I am she, but she too is part memory, part reconstruction, guesswork. Past selves, like familiar strangers.

I am sitting at the piano, fingers on the keyboard, head turned toward the camera, smiling broadly; I am curled up on the daybed in my parents' bedroom, leaning on one elbow with an illustrated book open before me, smiling; I am looking at myself in a mirror and seem to like what I see: my head is turned

away from the camera, but my face is visible in the mirror and I'm smiling. The next photo is equally artificial but more arresting. I sit at the edge of a wicker chair against a bare white wall illuminated by a halo of light from the photographer's lamp, my legs crossed at the ankles, my body slightly turned, head tilted, lips open in a melancholy smile. The pose is almost too grown-up, like one of those "waif" photos of starlets where the seduction is in the wistfulness, but the white knee socks and the slightly scuffed ankle-high lace-up shoes are those of a child.

Finally, there is a close-up, no props: a round-faced little girl with deep-set dark eyes and big ears, her eyebrows tensed in a barely visible frown. She looks at the camera, but her eyes seem turned inward. And despite all her finery—the bows, the hand-sewn flowers, the gold necklace and heart-shaped locket resting on the front of her dress—she looks sad. Is the sad little face the true one, the smiles merely superficial posing for the camera? Maybe it was just a passing shadow on an otherwise unclouded childhood.

Unclouded childhood. *Mommy, where are you going? Mommy, don't leave me!* The farm was for my safety and it wouldn't be for long, she said before she disappeared. *If I don't get used to this, I'll die.* By the time she came to get me again, a few weeks later, I looked like all the other kids, squatting barefoot in the dusty courtyard, playing. *Don't bother me now, I don't need you, don't kiss me.* She hugged me and hugged me, yet I felt nothing. How could I be sure that she would never leave me again? How can anyone be sure that those they love won't leave them?

After the war was finally over, it was the good time: we were all together again, Mother, Daddy, Granny, and I. And Uncle Laci too, who showed up at the door one afternoon, back from forced labor, a few weeks after we returned to our apartment,. "I made it," he announced with a broad grin, his face grimy above the tattered jacket. Laci, always smiling, the jovial one. (His older brother, Izsó, the serious one, never came back.)

Then everything returned to normal, except that whole families had been wiped out: Daddy's aunts and uncles and cous-

ins in Poland, Mother's uncles and aunts and cousins in the provinces in Hungary. But I didn't know about those people for many years—no one talked about them, at least not when I was around. I was busy with school, happily learning to read. Mother would buy me books about a girl named Zsuzsi, who had many adventures. I too had had an adventure, with Mother and

Daddy. We had escaped the Nazis, clever us! Hitler was dead; we had survived. Even Granny had survived in the ghetto where many died. What was there to be sad about?

A few years ago, on a visit to Budapest, I was taken up to the top floor of the synagogue on Dohány Street by a young researcher on the Holocaust. This was the office where historical records were kept, full of bookcases that looked badly in need of dusting. A lone archivist sitting at a cluttered desk kept watch; my friend introduced me to her. When she heard that I had lived in Budapest after the war, she pulled down a thick volume and handed it to me. I opened it to the title page: *Counted Remnant: Register of the Jewish Survivors in Budapest,* Budapest 1946. Below the date, the sponsors: "Published by the Hungarian Section of the World Jewish Congress and the Jewish Agency for Palestine Statistical and Search Department." A brief introduction informs the reader that this book "is one of gladness and of pain"—gladness at publishing the names of survivors, pain at the many thousands who did not survive. Of the roughly six hundred thousand Jews living in Hungary in 1944, more than two-thirds had perished by the time the Soviet army entered Budapest in January 1945. The Jews in the provinces were almost completely wiped out; the survivors were almost all in Budapest. The introduction goes on to explain that the counting began on July 8 and involved door to door visits by 402 "conscriptors" to more than thirty-five thousand houses in the capital: the surviving remnant was literally counted, one by one. There follows an alphabetical list of close to fourteen hundred pages, each page printed in two columns. Every survivor is listed by name (both married name and maiden name for women), place and year of birth, mother's maiden name, and current address in Budapest.

Naturally, I turn to the Rs first. Many Rubins appear there, including my grandparents Baruch and Esther, my favorite aunt—my father's younger sister Rózsi, who had not yet married—and my own parents: Rubin I. Miklós, born in Gorlice in 1910, and his wife Livia (she preferred it to her real name, Lilly, though no one called her Livia), maiden name Stern, born in Nyiregyháza in 1910. Gorlice is in Galizia, southern Poland, which had been part of the Habsburg Empire until 1919. My father's parents had settled in Budapest years before he was born, but his mother returned to her native town to give birth to her first child. Nyiregyháza, my mother's birthplace, is in northeastern Hungary, where some of her uncles and their families lived until they were deported to Auschwitz. Mother and her sister and brothers spent many summer vacations there, and evidently Granny was there the summer Lilly was born—July 1908, not 1910. Mother put the wrong date on every official document she had a chance to—she didn't want it known that she was two years older than her husband.

It takes me a while to realize that my name is missing from the list. A Rubin Zsuzsa is listed, but she was born in 1924 and her mother's name is no relation to mine. I look up and down the page several times, in case I appear in a different place among the Rubins, after Pál or Tekla or Simon—but no, my absence from the counted remnant is definitive. How could the conscriptors have seen my parents and grandmother, and even my uncle, all of them listed at the same address (Granny and Laci appear under the Sterns), and missed me? The introduction to the book warned that mistakes were inevitable—obviously, I was a mistake. But I can't help wondering: What if my absence from the list actually meant I had not survived? Only eleven percent of Jewish children alive at the outbreak of the war were still alive at its end, historians say. One out of nine. Statistically, I could have been—should have been, in terms of mere numbers—among the eight who did not make it, the unlucky ones.

It does feel a bit odd, though, to think that I was alive but not counted. Does that small human error have a deeper significance? Some survivors of the Holocaust have called themselves "revenants," ghosts, as if they had died and only their semblance returned to life. I have never thought of myself in that melodramatic way; in fact, I have hardly thought of myself as a survivor, with its connotations of trauma and suffering. I was just a small child during the war, and except for the time on the farm, my little world had remained intact—that's what I would have said, if anyone had asked me. But no one asked, and for a long time the notion of "child survivor" never entered my consciousness—or that of most people, for that matter. Later, I wrote extensively about child survivors, very rarely mentioning that I too could be counted as one. Maybe the conscriptors' error foreshadowed that denial.

Granny Rézi, Mother's mother, had lived with us ever since I could remember, and it was the same after the war. In her bedroom, on the wall above the bed, were two large photographs in twin frames: Rézi and her husband, Grandpa Stern, who had died many years before I was born. Stiff, unsmiling, dressed in their bourgeois best, the couple dominated the room. Rézi had brought up five children after her husband died, leaving her a young widow. By the time I knew her she was ageless, her whole person summed up in the role of grandmother. Small, round, vain, meddlesome, loving me to death, she would watch from the balcony every morning as I left for school and wait there for my return at one p.m. If I was late, dawdling with the other girls, she would get anxious, then angry. One day in first grade, in the autumn after the war, when I had dawdled with my friends longer than usual (we were talking about how babies are made), she scolded me loudly: she had been about to call the police when I showed up. I, big mouth, told her to stop acting like a policeman herself. Did she punish me for that freshness? No, she told the story of my clever repartee for years, as proof of my exceptional intelligence! That's why I forgave her all her meddling, because she loved me so much.

In the spring of 1948, Granny left us. She and Uncle Laci were emigrating, leaving Hungary forever. I kept repeating that sentence, without really understanding what it meant. Did people just leave their homes like that? Uncle Nick, Granny's youngest son, had left Hungary as a teenager and now lived in America and was rich. He was the one who had told them to leave. A few months earlier, he had sent all the necessary papers and money for the trip. He also sent me a ballpoint pen, which was a big hit in school because none of the other girls had one. We still wrote with pens we dipped into inkwells on our desks, and often made blotches on the page if we weren't careful to let the ink drip off first. The ballpoint pen began to leak after a few days and I had to throw it away, but Uncle Nick retained all his glamor, especially when he sent us a package of bananas. I had never seen a banana, and took one to school the next day. The teacher peeled it and carefully sliced it into small circles, handing each of us a piece. It was hardly enough to get more than a taste, but we all agreed that bananas were good.

Granny and Uncle Laci left in March, when the weather was still blustery. Granny wore her good winter coat and black hat. We went to see them off at the Eastern Station. She hugged me very close, crying, but I was too excited to respond in kind. I had never taken a big train, only the little subway under Andrássy Avenue and the cog railway up Sváb Mountain, where we went hiking on Sundays. This one had a big black locomotive and would take them to Paris! My aunt Magdi lived there, Mother's sister, and her husband Uncle Béla and my cousin Agnes, who was thirteen. I had never met them, but they would

soon be coming to visit us for the summer. Granny and Uncle Laci
planned to spend a few days with them in Paris, then take a big
boat to New York, where Uncle Nick would be waiting for them.

Granny sent us a photo from Paris, standing with Aunt
Magdi on a bridge right in front of the Eiffel Tower. I missed
her. She had made all my favorite noodle dishes, and practiced
the Shema with me every night until I knew the whole prayer
by heart, not just the first sentence everybody knows. She and
Mother often yelled at each other when Mother wasn't yelling
at Daddy, but I knew it wasn't serious, just the way families are,
always yelling and getting excited over things. They would often

have fights about me, and Uncle Laci joined in too. The child is too thin, she's not eating enough. Leave her alone, she knows when she's full. Give her cod liver oil, force it down if you have to. No, give her things she likes, chestnut purée with whipped cream. She reads too much, doesn't get enough exercise. Give her ballet lessons, they'll be good for her posture, she slumps too much. I felt as if they never took their eyes off me.

With Granny and Uncle Laci gone, there were no more fights like that; but I realized, obscurely, that I had enjoyed being the center of so much attention.

During the summer that followed Granny's departure, I turned nine and I fell in love—that was the only way to think of it, really. My cousin Agnes was blond, four years older than I, and lived in the fabled city of Paris; the minute I set eyes on her, I knew she could say or do no wrong. I did not speak French, but she spoke Hungarian well. I became her willing slave, she my benevolent idol. The philosopher Montaigne, mourning his soul mate and best friend Étienne de La Boétie, who had died of the plague while still young, explained their love for each other by a tautology: "because it was I, because it was he." That's how I felt about Agnes. The fact that each of us had grown up as an only child may have contributed to our bonding. We became like sisters, without the bitterness of sibling rivalry.

Agnes and Aunt Magdi and Uncle Béla were with us for two months, sharing the house we rented in a resort near the city. They had left Budapest in 1935, shortly after Agnes was born; Magdi and Mother had been best friends as well as sisters, and their reunion was a thing of joy. I took to Magdi too, immediately—she was calm and funny, not excitable like Mother. *Lilly gets hysterical, but Magdi has a sense of humor.* She would often talk about how she and Uncle Béla and Agnes had hidden in the south of France during the war, and she made it sound like a time of happiness and laughter, not fear. They and a few other refugees from Paris had formed a little society that met in the local café every night—but I may have imagined that, as part of my idea of a good time. Béla had fought in the French army as a foreign volunteer, and after France's defeat in 1940 he found himself in the southwest, along with two other Hungarian Jews in his group. They bought a dilapidated farm, and Magdi and Agnes managed to join them from Paris. The government had demanded that all Jews register and get a big *J* stamped on their identity cards, but they knew better than to follow that order. There was no electricity or indoor plumbing at the farm, but they made it work somehow. Béla enjoyed talking with the local farmers about their crops, about the woods around the village, the river where they cast for trout. He had grown up in a small town in Transylvania where he had learned to fish and hunt as a child. None of the farmers had ever seen a Jew, and this Parisian who spoke French with an accent but was familiar with their ways didn't correspond to their idea of one.

Béla and Magdi sent Agnes to a nearby village to school, and since it was too far from the farm to make the trip every day, they arranged for her to spend the week with an old mademoiselle, returning to the farm on weekends. Agnes lived that way for several years, shuttling between Mademoiselle and her parents. Mademoiselle was kind to her; she never pinched her. In Paris after the war, Magdi often pinched her when she was angry, leaving black and blue marks on her arm. Agnes told me these stories during our long nights awake in the room we shared. My image of Magdi became a bit tarnished when I heard about her pinching, but I still liked her. And while they were with us, she did not pinch at all.

The summer house was next to a large swimming club,

which had three different pools and a shaded terrace where you could have lunch. Agnes and I took swimming lessons, and after a couple of weeks we felt like pros. We would jump into the deep end of the pool feet first, sink to the bottom, then slowly float to the surface, scramble out, and start over. "Look at us, look at us!" we would yell to the grown-ups sitting on the terrace. Afterward, we would join them and play endless games of Monopoly, just the two of us. There were many other children there that summer, but we barely noticed them; we were living in a cocoon for two. In the evenings, a live orchestra played foxtrots and waltzes and tangos. The grown-ups sat at tables surrounding the dance floor, drinking colorful drinks and playing cards and gossiping. Occasionally, my father would get up and dance with us, but usually we danced with each other. Agnes led, I followed.

Toward the end of the summer, the club organized a dance recital: any child who signed up could do a five-minute solo. It was a real performance, with rehearsals. Agnes did a waltz to "The Blue Danube," I a mazurka to Chopin. A photo shows the two of us in our costumes, wearing lipstick for the occasion. Agnes has on a long gauzy dress with a satin belt around her waist, one arm around my shoulder, the other holding up her skirt to show off its width. I am wearing a short white dress that ends at my thighs, with long wide sleeves cinched at the wrists and a flouncy skirt outlined in red piping, a fantasy version of a Cossack outfit. (Did Cossacks do the mazurka? Never mind, it's Slavic.) On my head is a tall white fur hat, set at an angle over dark curls that cascade down past my shoulders. To finish off the Cossack theme, I'm wearing knee-high white boots—in reality, slip-on tops made of oilcloth, cut to fit over my shoes. Mother and I had run all over town to get those booties made in time for the show. I still remember the frantic race to pick them up that afternoon, our fear that we'd be late getting back, the adrenaline rush, as if our life depended on it. Once before,

I had felt that way—when Mother and I had left our house in Pest, after the Nazis came. Don't look right or left, look straight ahead—walk fast, don't run, act as if you have a right to be here. She had torn off her yellow star, holding my hand fast. When we got to the corner, we finally started to run. Did the panic come from that memory, or were we just overwrought females running after the perfect outfit?

A few days after the dance recital, we were awakened in the middle of the night. The ambulance was at the door and took Mother to the hospital, along with Daddy, who accompanied her. I spent a couple of nights alone with Aunt Magdi and Uncle Béla and Agnes. It was a miscarriage, and not her first one. No one told me anything; even Agnes couldn't say much. I had to guess it all. Being a woman is dangerous. Sometimes she's fat, sometimes thinner. Fat means hospital, tears, screaming. Wanting a baby, losing the baby. Wanting a boy. A boy had been born two years earlier, but he had died after one day. Many years later, her happiness when my own boys were born: "You did what I couldn't do," as if it were a question of talent. Why was it better to have a boy, to be a boy? She grew up in Freud's world, Vienna-Budapest. What does a woman want?

When Mother came out of the hospital, we moved back to the city. A few days later, Agnes and her parents returned to Paris, and I took to my bed like a bereaved widow. The previous year, when I had had the measles, I had spent long days in bed reading and enjoying time off from school, basking in the special attentions of Mother and Granny as they brought me hot chocolate and candy and other little presents. This was different, a deadly sadness that made me unable to think of anything except the pain I was feeling. But it was not pain, exactly—rather, a kind of numbness. Granny, Laci, Agnes,

Magdi, all gone. Suddenly, I felt the full weight of those departures, as if everyone I loved had disappeared without warning. Emptiness. *If I don't get used to this, I'll die.*

Freud speaks of mourning and melancholia, human re-actions to loss. Mourning eventually comes to an end, while melancholy is endless. For the first few days, it felt as if I would never get up, never leave my bed, lie forever curled up in a ball, staring at the wall. Mother tried to cheer me up, but I just lay there. Then, gradually, I began to revive. School was starting; there were books. Around that time, Mother took me to the children's dressmaker and ordered the light blue wool dress.

Years later, whenever I saw Agnes in New York or Miami, I would remember that summer and the devastation that followed, and wonder how I could now feel only ordinary affection for her, when then I had missed her so much I thought I would die.

4

Red Bicycle

I have no photographs of Pista, my first love outside the family. That may be because I did not know him very well, and because he died when he was ten years old. Pista is the diminutive of István, a name much favored by Hungarians. St. István (aka St. Stephen), Hungary's first Christian king, who reigned around the year 1000, has an imposing basilica named after him in Budapest—yet despite his sainthood, his name is ecumenical. Around 1939, Hungarian Jews who would never have dreamed of calling their children Attila or Csaba, names from the pre-Christian Magyar conquest that carried ugly nationalist overtones, had no qualms at all about calling their sons István. On the contrary, they flocked to the name—maybe because it was a way of declaring their love of Hungary without treading on the antisemites' ground.

At any rate, István was that boy's name and everyone called him Pista, or even more affectionately, Pistuka. He had ruddy cheeks, dark brown hair, a slender body. I dreamed about him often. Our parents were friends—more exactly, he and his parents and my mother and I often teamed up with others for family hikes in the Buda hills on Sundays. My father did not go on those hikes, pretexting work. The rest of us set out early in the morning, fall, winter, and spring—in the summer, everyone went to Lake Balaton or other places with water. We would meet at the terminal of the cog railway on the Buda side, then pile into the rickety wagon and ride to the top. There, we opened our thermoses and drank hot lemon tea, after which the kids ran around while the adults sat chatting on wooden benches. A series of wide open hills were our playground, snow-covered in winter, perfect for sledding; at other times, for playing tag. Below us stretched the city, with its imposing monuments and bridges, but up here we were in the wilderness. After our lunch of sand-wiches and hard-boiled eggs, with strips of salted green pepper, we would all gather and walk down on the well-marked trails, the kids running ahead, circling back at intervals to check on their parents. Sometimes, in winter, darkness was falling by the time we reached the bottom, where everyone took their streetcar or bus home and promised to return the following Sunday.

Pista laughed a lot, and everyone liked him. But I dreamed of kissing him, spending long days with him, marrying him! I was nine, he was ten. Already then, I was extremely shy about declaring my feelings to a member of the opposite sex, so my fantasies remained unknown to him, unless my mooning looks gave them away. He never showed the slightest interest in me, other than as one of the kids.

In the spring of 1949, Pista died in an automobile ac-cident that his parents survived with minor scratches. He was riding in the passenger seat next to his father and didn't wear a seat belt—there weren't any, in those days. Thrown against the windshield, which had shattered, he bled to death when his jugular vein was sliced by a piece of broken glass. By the time the ambulance arrived, it was all over.

At first, the grown-ups didn't want to tell us kids, but there was no way to keep it from us. It was the only thing they talked about for weeks and weeks, on Sundays. Why was Pista riding in front, and not his mother? Could his parents have done anything to stop the bleeding while they were waiting for the ambulance? If the ambulance had reached them earlier, would he have survived? Everyone had an opinion, repeated over and over. "The worst is for the parents," that was universally agreed on. Pista had been their only child, the light of their eyes. "They keep consulting doctors, asking whether Pista would have lived if they had gotten him to the hospital more quickly." Everyone nodded: the worst was for the parents, they would never get over it.

To have survived the war, the Nazis, the Arrow Cross, and then lose their child in a senseless accident! Fate was too cruel (no one mentioned God). I suddenly understood what it was to lose someone for real—not in a teary goodbye, like when Granny or my cousin Agnes left us, but forever. The finality of that word: for ever.

If only, if only . . . I played a film in my head as I went to sleep every night. The blood is spurting from Pista's neck, but the ambulance people put a bandage on it and he is saved, and soon we are back on our hikes as if nothing had happened.

Why are some people lucky, surviving against all odds, while others die?

Before Pista, I had lost a little brother. He lived for only one day, born with a defective heart—a blue baby, the doctors said. He was born in August 1946: the war was over and the future looked hopeful. I stayed with my father's two sisters, my aunts Betty and Rózsi, while Mother and Daddy went to the hospital. In the middle of the night, we were woken up by my father's cry from the street: "It's a boy!" He and Mother had always wanted a boy. He was ecstatic, and so were we. "You have a little brother, dearest Zsuzsika," Rózsi said, hugging me. His name was András, and I would soon be able to see him.

But I never did, for by the next day he was dead. It was not even enough time to miss him, really. My parents never talked about him after that, at least not in my presence. But the blow was enormous, I now realize. The accepted wisdom in such cases is "Try again as soon as you can." A series of miscarriages followed, until the premature birth and almost miraculous survival of my sister four years later. By then, simply having a living baby made up for the lack of a boy.

When I was in Budapest some years ago, I found baby András's name inscribed in the registry of births at the Orthodox Community Bureau. I recognized my father's careful handwriting; part of his job at the bureau was to keep track of births and deaths. The baby had no Hebrew name; he had died too quickly for that. He should not have been inscribed in the registry at all, according to Jewish law, but Daddy must have gotten some comfort from writing his name and the dates—proof that he had existed.

In the spring of 1949, a few weeks after Pista died, my father went into the hospital for minor surgery. He had been suffering from an ulcer for years, and the doctor advised him to have it removed. Ulcers were the result of too much worrying, everyone said. Daddy had certainly had his share of worries during the war—and since then, the daily shouting matches with Mother were not much help, I thought. He would turn thirty-nine in a few months, still a young man. Better get it out now, the doctor told him.

The operation went smoothly, but the day before he was due to come home from the hospital, he had a massive heart attack. Mother rushed to his bedside and was told the chances for his survival were fifty-fifty. He asked her to bring one of his Talmudic books to place under his pillow. She made a vow that if God allowed him to recover, she would cut her hair and wear a shaytl, the wig worn by Orthodox married women. That had long been a sore point in their marriage: she had refused to cut her beautiful black hair. I don't know just how important it was to him personally—if it had truly mattered to him, he could have married a rabbi's daughter instead of a headstrong "modern" woman like my mother. But her refusal made him feel ashamed in front of his father, a stern patriarch who had not forgiven him for marrying a woman without a dowry, a woman who was not even religious enough to compensate for her lack of money. This time, she was willing to make the sacrifice: God could have her hair if He saved her husband.

For several weeks, she practically lived at the hospital, leaving home early in the morning and returning late at night. Oddly, I cannot recall who stayed with me, or if anyone did. I must have gone to school every day, but I have no memory of that either. Yet big changes had been going on there, because all the parochial schools in Hungary had been nationalized the previous summer—a sign of the increasing power of the Communist Party. In my school, a girls' elementary school attached to the Orthodox Community Bureau, we now wear navy blue skirts and white blouses with red string ties, as junior members of the Young Pioneers. For one school celebration, I learn a poem by the national poet Sándor Petőfi, who died young in the failed 1848 revolution against Habsburg rule. The poem's title and inflammatory refrain is "Hang All the Kings!," which I belt out with great fervor. I would no doubt have become a passionate young communist if we had remained in Hungary, I sometimes tell myself. I have even spun out scenarios: I fight heroically, along with other communist reformers, in the 1956 revolution, and after the crackdown I struggle over whether to leave Hungary or stay and face the consequences. I leave with my boyfriend and we settle in Paris. I stay in Budapest and lose all faith in communism; I am sent to prison, even though I am still a teenager. Et cetera. (People living in Central Europe have had a lot of capital-H History to contend with, over the past century.)

It's strange that I have so little precise memory of those weeks while my father was in the hospital—after all, I was almost ten years old. Most likely, it was Madame, the Viennese lady who taught me French, who took care of me during the hours while Mother was at the hospital. She picks me up at school, and we take our usual detour to walk down Andrássy Avenue, stopping to buy a cone of chestnut purée topped with whipped cream on the way home. One day, coming toward us on the sidewalk, I see a girl wheeling a shiny red bicycle—she looks happy, guiding the bike along as she talks with a woman walking next to her, probably her mother. After they pass us, I turn around to stare at them, unsure whether it is the beautiful bike or the happy girl that attracts me. Madame asks me what I am looking at, but I don't answer.

One thing I remember with certainty is that I knew my father was in danger of dying. Death is forever. My handsome, brilliant father must not die! I think I prayed for him, though I am not sure of that either. At night I would lie in bed, immobile, waiting for my mother to return. As long as she was home, I knew he was still alive.

The Talmudic book under his pillow and Mother's bargain with God did their job, apparently. Daddy was finally allowed to leave the hospital. But he had to be very careful, the doctor said: no climbing stairs, no smoking, lots of rest. I was waiting downstairs, and when they arrived in the taxi I leaped at him, wanting to hug him. "Gently," he said, avoiding my arms. His face was drawn; he looked like an invalid. We lived three long flights up and our building had no elevator, but Mother had arranged for two strong men to carry him upstairs. They joined hands and had him sit with one arm around each man's neck. He would not be able to leave the apartment until he could navigate those stairs alone. It hurt me to see him so helpless, he who had always been my hero.

Mother cut her hair and bought a wig, which she wore for a few months. After he was better and her hair had started to grow back, she gave it up. She hadn't told God how long she would wear the wig, so she felt she had kept her promise. Daddy, for his part, hosted a dinner of thanksgiving in our dining room, to which he invited about a dozen Talmudic scholars. For weeks he prepared and then rehearsed his speech, in Yiddish, with me as his audience. It was a disquisition on Maimonides, the medieval sage who is often referred to as the Rambam. I couldn't understand a word of it, having no knowledge of Yiddish (that was another sore point between my parents—he spoke it with his parents and other religious Jews, while she disdained it), but "Rambam" sounded extraordinarily comical to my ears, and I went into elaborate performances of hilarity every time he pronounced the word. He would smile at me indulgently, and that made me want to perform even more, although after a while I no longer found it funny. I wanted his approval, wanted him to look at me and smile. It was around that time, I think, that I began to turn against my mother, as if it were impossible to love them both at the same time.

There is a photo of that dinner, showing ten men dressed in dark suits around the table in our dining room—the table is spread with a white cloth and the moment is after the meal, when only the glasses and decanters are left. One or two of the men have beards, others are clean-shaven or wear a mustache; a few sit with their backs toward the camera, so all one sees of their head is the hat. The hats are the giveaway that this is an

Orthodox gathering; more assimilated Jews would not sit around a dining table wearing fedoras. My father and a couple of others wear yarmulkes instead, but the hats dominate the picture. The only one standing is Daddy—evidently he is about to give his after-dinner speech about the Rambam. I am not there to admire him this time; the dinner is an all-male affair.

I fish out another photo from the pile—this one is in sepia, a copy of a much older picture that my aunt Rózsi must have sent to Mother after Daddy died. It shows another group around a table, a small round table with nothing but a patterned dark cloth on it—probably a prop in the photographer's studio, for this is a highly posed picture taken by a professional. My father, his four sisters, and his parents are formally arrayed. This time it's Daddy who wears a black hat, while his father wears a large skullcap. The young man sits with one arm resting on the table; although he is wearing a dark suit and the hat, he appears to be a teenager, no more than eighteen or nineteen years old. His clothes tell us that he is a *yeshiva bocher*, a student of the Talmud, the pride of the family. His younger sister Rózsi, who is about ten, stands close to him and has placed her hand on his arm, as if to draw him even closer; the littlest girl, Ica, is seated next to Rózsi, looking bored. The two older girls, Hera and Betty, stand on the other side of him, each with one hand resting on the table; next to them are the parents, seated. My grandmother, a solid-looking woman, wears a patterned dress with a white collar. Her hair is carefully waved, evidently a wig; she is unadorned, except for a long, thin gold necklace from which a small locket spills onto her dress. My grandfather, a handsome man in a three-piece suit, has a white beard, but his mustache is still dark. His eyes are just like my father's, dark and deeply set beneath well-defined eyebrows.

The whole family looks solemn, even glum, except for Rózsi, who is smiling slightly and looks lively. I allow myself to fantasize about the occasion for this photo. Moshe, the firstborn and the only son, has been home from his yeshiva and is about to leave again to finish his studies; he is dressed for the trip, wearing what is almost a uniform, dark suit and dark hat. Or maybe he has just returned from the yeshiva, and the family is marking the occasion by getting dressed up and going to the photographer. Either way, my sense is that he is now a bit of a stranger in his family, like a visiting dignitary. But that may be a projection on my part.

I wish I knew exactly where that yeshiva was, and what brand of Orthodoxy it belonged to. But the only one who could tell me, my aunt Rózsi, died more than ten years ago. I found an old doctoral dissertation on microfilm, which listed every yeshiva operating in Hungary between the two world wars. They were all outside Budapest, 84 of them, and that's counting only those that had remained within Hungary's borders after World War I. Another 139 had ended up as part of Romania or Czechoslovakia. This proliferation was unique to Hungary, the author writes. The particular character of each yeshiva depended on the rabbi who was in charge. Some were run by Hasidic *rebbes*, others not; but they were all ultra-Orthodox, offering an exclusively religious course of study untainted by secular subjects. The suit my father wears in the photo, with a white shirt and tie, is not typical of the Hasidic sects, for they wear long black caftans and no ties. His hat, however, a black felt homburg, is often worn by Hasidic men on weekdays instead of the elaborate fur hats they wear on special occasions. But I don't see any *payes* on him, the sidelocks of Hasidic Jews, and his father doesn't have them either. Moshe does sport a small, stylish mustache and a hint of a beard. Conflicting signals, in the end.

Wherever it was that my father attended the yeshiva, family legend has it that his father sent him there after the boy lost the gold watch he had received from an American cousin for his bar mitzvah, in a spirited game of after-school street soccer. He had taken off the watch to keep it safe and left it near his jacket and school bag, but when he looked for it after the game, it was gone. The loss of the watch persuaded Yehoshuah Baruch that his son Moshe was becoming spoiled by the secular ways of the big city. He himself had emigrated to Budapest from Gorlice, a city in Galizia in southern Poland, around 1900, when that whole region was still part of the Austro-Hungarian Empire. A few years later he married a girl from his hometown, and in 1910 his wife Esther returned to Gorlice temporarily and gave birth to their son.

Yehoshuah Baruch was a modest tailor by profession, but in the Jewish religious hierarchy he occupied a very high rank— he was a *cohen*, a direct descendant of the high priest of the

Temple in Jerusalem. And to add to that distinction, his wife was the daughter of a *cohen*, a status that carries its own designation: *bat cohen*. Since the *cohen* title was transmitted through male children, my father's position as the only son made his father all the more determined to keep him in the Orthodox fold. (It also explains, in part, why my parents were so eager to have a son.) So Yehoshuah Baruch packed his son off to the provincial yeshiva, where the boy would be far from secular temptations. In due course, Moshe earned the title of rabbi and his father expected him to marry a rabbi's daughter—a modest girl, preferably not poor, with good connections among the Orthodox elite.

It did not work out that way. My mother, Lilly, although she had been brought up in a kosher household, was far from the ideal that Yehoshuah Baruch had in mind for his son. Lilly loved parties, theater, the pastry shops on Andrássy Avenue, and the fancy baths and open-air pools at the Gellért Hotel, where young people rendezvoused on Sundays. In her, my father found all the attractions of Budapest that he had missed during his yeshiva years. His father never forgave him for it.

Moshe and Lilly had met not long after he returned to the city, around 1933, in the office of the Orthodox Community Bureau, where he had gotten a job as a midlevel administrator; she went there every afternoon to deliver the receipts from the kosher butcher shop where she worked as a cashier. Her father had run a prosperous dry-goods business, but after his premature death from a stroke when she was fifteen, the family had fallen on hard times. Lilly was in her midtwenties when they met, two years older than Moshe—or rather Miklós, for she preferred the Hungarian version of his name. This went hand-in-hand with her disdain for Yiddish, the language of choice in his family. The disdain went both ways, of course. When I was growing up, I almost never saw my paternal grandmother or grandfather—they were like strangers, people we paid stiff visits to. I adored my aunt Rózsi, my father's sister, but in my mind she occupied a different space, separate from theirs. She was the one who told me, after Mother died, that their marriage had caused a huge rift with his father. In fact, they had gotten married secretly, fearing the old man's wrath, and continued for a while to live separately, each with their family. Later, when they had a public wedding, my grandfather refused to attend. He finally relented, Rózsi told me, but he kept his grudge.

My parents' formal wedding photo hangs on a wall in my apartment: she a dark-haired beauty in a white satin dress, holding a large bouquet of white roses on her lap, he dapper in tails, sporting a white bow tie, holding a top hat and gloves on his knee. One would hardly know, looking at that photo, that they came from modest Jewish families whose members never had occasion to dress that way in real life. But it's the secret marriage, so romantic, that intrigues me and sets me dreaming. How passionately they must have loved each other!

During the months I spent in Budapest in 1993, I hunted down their official marriage certificate. It was dated July 21,

1936: she would be twenty-eight the following week, and he had turned twenty-six the previous month. For close to a year, they kept the marriage secret. My dream focuses on him: At night after his parents and sisters are in bed, he tiptoes out of the apartment and down the stairs, then steps onto the dark avenue and turns right toward the Oktogon. The Lukács café is black and silent, like all the other buildings at this late hour. He likes these nightly walks alone, even in cold weather like now. A few hours later, he will make the same trip in the other direction, watching the sun rise as he sneaks back home. He and Lilly have been married for six months, and nobody knows except her mother—they had to tell her, otherwise she wouldn't let him come each night. She keeps asking him when he will tell his parents, but the time is not right yet. The old man would take it hard. Just that morning, he had cornered him before he left for work: "You're a *cohen* on both sides," he said for the thousandth time. "Marry that nice girl and within a year you'll be her father's chief assistant. After he goes, you'll become the *rebbe*. Do our family proud." The old man has a fearsome temper. If he found out about the marriage, watch out! Penniless orphan, paints her nails, not a single *cohen* in the family. Miklós turns up his collar and digs his hands into his coat pockets. Soon he will be warm in Lilly's bed. Beautiful blue-eyed Lil, his laughing wife, her hair like cedars of Lebanon, her teeth like white heifers on Mount Carmel. The Song of Songs finally makes sense, but the yeshiva did not prepare him for this pleasure—the sweetness of it, every night. He feels his flesh rise as he thinks about her, his blood rushing as he quickens his steps. The pale-faced rabbi's daughter will have to find herself another groom.

By falling in love with Lilly, my father revealed (or chose) a doubleness in his person and his loyalties that would remain with him for the rest of his life. Was he a soulful Talmudic scholar uninterested in the material temptations life offered, or a bon vivant with an eye for beautiful women? I think he was both, which means he could not be fully either one; or let's say he could not bend either way without some regret for the other, occasionally accompanied by a deep sense of irony. One day, years after we had left Hungary, he asked me to accompany him to an Orthodox wedding in Brooklyn. I was in college by then, and he must have been visiting from Chicago, without my mother. I knew no one at the wedding, but he knew many people—I assumed they were old connections, from his yeshiva days or from the Orthodox Community Bureau. After the ceremony, there was dancing: the men, all dressed in black suits except for my father, who wore a gray one, danced in one room while the women danced in the adjoining one. The door between them was open, and as I watched the men I caught my father's eye. He was moving with the others, slowly, but his face had a quizzical smile as he looked at me, as if to say *I appear slightly out of place, don't I? Yet I know these people, I could have been one of them. As it is, I am a visitor.* Maybe I am imagining that is what he meant. I do know that he never felt fully at peace, in one place or the other. Which may explain (at least in part) the ulcer, the heart attack at age thirty-nine, and his death before he reached fifty.

In the summer that followed the heart attack and the thanksgiving dinner, we moved out to a resort near where we had spent the joyous weeks with my cousin Agnes and her family a year earlier. The swimming club was still there and I still loved to jump off the deep end of the pool, but this time there were no visitors from Paris and the atmosphere at home was tense. Unbeknownst to me, my parents were planning our escape from Hungary. By then it had to be an escape, because exit visas were no longer granted. Even before the elections that fall, which officially brought the Communist Party to power, the country was effectively shut down by the Iron Curtain.

But that was beyond my ken. What mattered to me was that I desperately wanted a red bicycle for my tenth birthday. I had seen a girl about my age ride one near our house, and remembered the girl on Andrássy Avenue who had looked so happy wheeling hers. The bicycle was the color of cherries, with shiny chrome fenders and handlebars, the most beautiful thing I had ever seen. To ride on a bike like that would be sheer heaven, I was sure of it. I talked about it constantly, to my mother and Aunt Rózsi, who often joined us on weekends with her husband János. János, or Jancsi as everyone called him, came from an as-similated Jewish family, much higher on the social ladder than any of us. He was a handsome, powerful-looking man used to giving orders, but he could turn on the charm as well. He and his father owned a large lumber business, and Rózsi was his partner. She had an extraordinary head for business, everyone said—un-like her brother, the Talmudic scholar. Coming from a poor fam-ily, she had started to work early, and by the time János met her, just before the war, she had a good position at a rival firm. She refused his advances, knowing his reputation as a ladies' man, but after the war they connected again, became partners in the lumber company, and got married. My first memories of them together date from around that time, when they would come to our house and take me for rides on Jancsi's motorcycle. It was a big machine with a sidecar for passengers, where I sat, while she rode behind him. They both wore long leather trench coats, like characters in a postwar thriller. I didn't know about thrillers yet, but those coats enchanted me. They promised adventure.

In the summer there were no leather coats, but there was adventure. Jancsi owned a motorboat on which he took Rózsi and me for jaunts on the Danube, from a dock behind the house where we were staying. The boat had an outboard motor that had to be started by pulling on a rope, and it never worked the first time. The motor sputters, then dies out, and Jancsi utters melodramatic curses as he pulls at the rope. When he finally gets it going, he sits back, a big smile on his face, and we speed down the river. "Watch out for whirlpools," he yells above the noise of the motor, "they can put us into a spin and we'll never get out of it. As for swimming, they'll drag you to the bottom in an instant." None of us planned to swim in that water, but the thought that we might be caught in a whirlpool, utterly helpless, made the excursion even more exciting. We would arrive back at the house, triumphant, as if we had braved an enormous danger.

When July 18 came, I got my red bicycle—oh happiness! It had a metal basket in the front, and a little bell on the handlebar that made a loud tinkling sound. Get of my way, I'm here! When I was on that bike, I felt all was right with the world. It was as if I owned the road.

Less than a month later, I had to leave the bicycle behind, along with everything else in that life: the apartment on Acacia Street with its proud balcony overlooking the street, my school and its red neckties, the chestnut purees of Andrássy Avenue, the hills of Buda, the memory of the boy I had loved and who died.

Part II

In Transit

5

Traveling Chess Set

In preparation for our departure from Hungary, my father bought a miniature chess set, the kind used by travelers. The tiny chess pieces had pegs on the bottom, inserted into holes in the middle of each square; to move a piece, you lifted it out and stuck it in another hole. When not in use, the board folded in half and became a box for storing the pieces; an ingenious little metal hook kept the box closed.

I had just turned ten and was eager to play with my father. He taught me the basic moves and the opening gambit, where both players move two pawns forward, facing each other, and then proceed to exchange one for one. That leaves the board open for long treks by the bishops, threatening the opposing king—after that the game gets going, as each player tries to attack and defend. I found it engrossing, and was proud to be able to prolong a game before my father said "Checkmate." We often laughed at that point. One of these days, I'd tell him, I was going to win. He would look at me with his soft, quizzical eyes: "Not for a while yet," he would say with a smile.

We used the chess set on winter evenings in Vienna that year, and on the boat that carried us across the Atlantic a few months later. We also played during the months we spent in Haiti, waiting for our visa to the States. Sitting across from my father, staring intently at the board and trying out one move after another in my head, I felt I was sharing something private and unique with him, reserved just for the two of us. We were both silent, concentrating on the game, but occasionally we exchanged a smile. How I loved my father, that deeply intelligent and handsome man!

Did he love me in return? Certainly, but not the way I dreamed of. I yearned to be beautiful in his eyes, but he did not see me as beautiful—maybe he had once, when I was a blond toddler. But now I was an awkward, chubby pre-adolescent with thick brown braids framing a round face—really not much to look at. Smart, yes; but not beautiful, not like my mother or the other women who caught his eye. (It's strange for me to think of him, with all his intellectualism, as a man with a roving eye. But from what I learned about him years later, I had to bow to the reality of his doubleness. As far as I know, there was never any serious threat to the marriage, but from early on he had a tendency to stray that provoked tantrums from my mother.) So I became what he saw me as, a girl with brains, a girl who read a lot, a girl who played chess. "You're beautiful and sexy, but you never lead with that," a lover once told me. It's true, I never lead with that. But then I think of Simone de Beauvoir, whose father told her when she was still in the lycée that she had better prepare herself to earn a living, since she had no dowry; implied was his assessment that she wasn't beautiful enough to marry without one. Beauvoir recalls that when she reached the "awkward age," her father ceased paying attention to her in favor of her pretty younger sister. All the photos of her as a young woman prove that she was beautiful, but I think she never believed it.

I still own the chess set—heaven knows how it survived all these years. The metal lock is gone and the hinge of the box is broken, replaced by a rubber band; the shiny finish of the little pieces has mostly worn off and some of the pieces are missing, making the set unusable. But the kings are there, and the queens and bishops and knights; as I hold the pieces in my hand, it strikes me that my father's fingerprints are on them somewhere. Of all my relics, this may be the one I prize the most. Catholics have pieces of the true cross; I have pieces of a chess set.

Our escape from Hungary was an adventure, though more exciting in the telling than in the living of it. I already told one version of our exit in *Budapest Diary*; here I will do so with a few other details, but the story is essentially the same. (This was one of the few memories I chose to remember during the many years when I forgot Budapest, although I still did not relate the story to my children or husband.)

On a hot August day, we walked out of our apartment on Acacia Street, carrying light suitcases and heading for the Western Station. It's all a blur, like so many of my memories from that time. The next thing I knew, we were off the train, sitting in a cornfield (all the stalks were gone, the field was bare and stubbly), waiting for the sun to set. Our guide told us we would cross freshly harvested fields into a village close to the Czechoslovak border, arriving there late at night when no one would see us; a local farmer would allow us to spend the night at his house. In the morning, we would board a bus to the city of Kosice. Kosice used to be Kassa, part of northeastern Hungary in the days of the empire. Hitler had given it back to Hungary during the war, but that was over now; Kosice, with its many Hungarian speakers, was in Czechoslovakia. The border was barely marked, the guide explained, and the guards almost never stopped the bus there. We had to count on that, since we had no papers allowing us to cross.

Our group grew a little as we waited; a boy traveling by himself, who could not have been more than fifteen, joined us. He was from Budapest and had already tried crossing the border once, he told us, but had been arrested and taken back to the city. Not a good sign, we thought, but at least he hadn't been jailed—they simply deposited him on the outskirts and let him go.

Almost as soon as we started walking, things began to go wrong. My father twisted his ankle on the stubbly field and limped all the way with gritted teeth, slowing us down. He found a stick to lean on, but I could tell each step was an agony. By the time we reached the village, it was dawn; dogs barked, roosters crowed—our arrival did not pass unnoticed. After a couple of hours' rest at the farmhouse, the guide took us to the road to wait for the bus. When it arrived, he introduced us to the driver, who spoke Hungarian; then he disappeared. Not to worry, the driver said, he would take good care of us. The bus had only a few passengers, who looked like they were traveling from local villages, the men wearing work clothes and sturdy boots, the women with kerchiefs on their heads, holding baskets on their lap. We sat down and started to doze.

Half an hour later, the bus screeches to a halt. Suddenly, we are wide awake. Two policemen get on—so much for never being stopped at the border, I say to myself. "Papers," they order, but we have none. The bus driver puts his arm around my mother and says she is his wife! All right, but what about the girl and boy and the man? They must get off, the policemen say. My eyes widen: *This is surely the end.* Daddy and I were escorted off the bus, along with our teenage companion, and taken into a small room. After a few minutes, another policeman entered and took me by the arm, wordlessly escorting me back to the bus. My mother had put up such a ruckus, crying and screaming for her child, that they had no choice but to come and get me if the bus was to leave. As to how I could be her child and the child of the man they had just taken off the bus, while she was also the driver's wife, no one bothered to ask. The whole thing appeared slightly comical, the officials playing a role whose script they had not yet learned properly, or that was still being written. Just a year earlier, Granny and Uncle Laci had left for Paris by getting on a train; that was no longer possible. From now on it was the Iron Curtain, but still in its amateurish stage. Except that it was also terrifying—and my father was no longer with us.

The bus moved on toward Kosice. Czechoslovakia was behind the Iron Curtain too, so why go there if we wanted to end up in Vienna? It didn't make sense, but none of it made sense. The stealthy departure from Budapest, the stubbly fields, Daddy's twisted ankle, the dogs barking in the village, the arrest, and my return to the bus all melded together into an incomprehensible jumble. Don't try to figure it out, just keep still and watch what is happening, as if it were happening to someone else. Psychologists call it dissociation, observing yourself from a distance, so that whatever pain or terror you might feel becomes separated from you. It's how abused children cope, or anyone who feels totally helpless or expects to die. I did not think I would die on that bus, but fearing that my world would fall apart was probably enough.

When we reached Kosice, Mother and I found our way to a large room filled with people sitting on the floor on mats—Jewish refugees on their way to the new land of Israel. My parents had evidently planned to join the group there, even though they had no intention of going to Israel. Daddy must have known about it through his work at the Orthodox Community Bureau, which would have been involved in organizing such exits. Mother showed herself once again to be a tough woman; she kept badgering the men in charge, begging them to "do something" about getting Daddy released so he could join us. I sat on a mat and waited.

Meanwhile, back at the police station, as Daddy later re-counted, he told the policemen he was a rabbi and asked if he could pray. Sure, they said. He got his *tefillin* out of his suitcase, strapped the small black box on his forehead and wrapped the thin leather straps around his arm, just as he did every morn-ing—the policemen had probably never seen anything like it. Then he started to pray, swaying back and forth the way Ortho-dox men do. Suddenly, he keeled over. The policemen rushed to him. "I had a heart attack a few months ago," he told them. Unsure of their script, the policemen looked at each other, then at him. Phone calls were made, and a few hours later he was transported out of there on a stretcher, on his way to Kosice. I suppose they didn't want a dead migrant on their hands.

Did he fake it, or did he really faint? He claimed he had faked it, but I could not be sure. At any rate, God was still smiling on him. He arrived on his stretcher in the middle of the night, waking everybody up. Our teenage traveling com-panion, he told us, had been sent back to Budapest again. But we ran into him in Vienna a few weeks later, living proof that persistence pays off, at least sometimes.

The next morning, we straggled out with the other refugees and took a train west, to Bratislava. My aunt Ica, Daddy's young-est sister, lived there with her husband, a doctor she had met during the war. They had both fought the Nazis as partisans in Czechoslovakia and were committed communists, until the trial and execution of Rudolf Slansky and other Jewish communist leaders a few years later proved to them that the revolution in Czechoslovakia, like all the others, ate its own children, espe-cially if they were Jews. After that, Aunt Ica and her husband seized the first opportunity to flee the country with their two boys, but back in 1949 they still had hopes for a new dawn right where they were. Still, she told us to get on the first train for Vienna. "Don't wait, just get out of here" was her advice to her brother, who had hoped to rest at her house for a few days. But the urgency in her voice left no room for doubt. He knew about a sealed train of Jewish refugees leaving that evening for Trieste, from where they would embark on a ship to Israel. The train would pass through Vienna, and we would get off some-how—yet another thing that made no sense until it happened.

Daddy faked another fainting session as the train neared Vienna and they took him off on a stretcher, with Mother and me in tow. He spent a night in the hospital while we stayed in a hotel nearby. Next thing I knew, we were living in a Viennese lady's apartment as subtenants; she rented us two rooms and we shared the kitchen. This was postwar Vienna, the Vienna of *The Third Man*, though that kind of intrigue was very far from us. Our Vienna was not a moody city with dark shadows but a once-great capital full of bombed-out houses that it was slowly rebuilding. Its past grandeur notwithstanding, the city was oc-cupied by the Allied powers until 1955, divided into sectors: American, French, British, Soviet. Our street, Lerchenfelder-strasse, was in the American sector, or maybe the French—it's a very long street, as I see on a current map. Why do I unhesitat-ingly remember the complicated name of Lerchenfelderstrasse, when I have forgotten so much else?

We were now officially stateless Jewish refugees fleeing from behind the Iron Curtain.

It soon became time for me to start school again. Just because we were marking time with no idea of where we would go next was no reason to deprive me of an education, my parents must have reasoned. On a sunny day in September, my father accompanied me to a Jewish school where a good part of the instruction was in Hebrew. The principal escorted me to a class that was already in session; the teacher, a friendly-looking man, pointed me to a seat next to another girl and went on with his lesson. I didn't understand a word, but suddenly I saw him standing in front of me, holding out an open box of apples arranged in neat rows. It looked like he was offering me one, so I reached in and took a shiny red apple. When I hear the class titter, I realize my mistake: the teacher was not asking me to take an apple but merely to admire them. I blush deeply and do my best not to cry. The apples were probably from Israel, proof of how the young country was creating farms out of the desert. After he had gone around the room displaying them, the teacher went around again; this time he took an apple out at every desk, cut it in half, and gave a piece to each of the girls sitting there. When he came to my desk, he cut the apple that was already there and gave half of it to the girl sitting next to me. He handed me my half gently, with a smile and no trace of mockery. But I felt too humiliated to appreciate his gesture. *Everyone is laughing at me!*

The rest of the day was a torment. I had always loved school and been a good student, even a teacher's pet. But here I didn't understand anything, and could not wait for the day to end. *Why am I here? Get me out!* When my father came to pick me up, I told him I never wanted to go back there again. I must have looked very determined, or very sad, because he did not insist.

After a couple of days, he registered me at the school in the French sector, staffed by teachers from France. I felt like a misfit there too, because the French I had learned from Madame in Budapest was barely more than rudimentary. But at least I knew something, and the wonders of the French school system, with its rigid rules where everything made sense, allowed me to feel I was progressing. I made no friends at the school, however. Most of the girls were children of French diplomats or military people attached to the occupying forces, and they didn't need the friendship of a lost-looking Hungarian girl. Mother had stopped rolling my hair into a "rooster's crown" atop my head, that uniquely Hungarian creation for little girls, but foreignness was stamped on my face like a postmark. *Will I ever fit in anywhere?* My classmates were foreigners too in Vienna, but they had a home they would return to, and France had been among the conquerors of Hitler. (No one spoke about Marshal Pétain and the Vichy regime, which had willingly collaborated with the Nazis; General de Gaulle had saved French honor.) I, on the other hand, was a refugee from the east, in transit to God knows where.

Not everything was negative about Vienna. Mother and Daddy seemed strangely happy, as if we were on an endless vacation. Mother learned to bake delicious pastries filled with a paste of walnuts and sugar, or with the sweet poppy seed mixture that is a staple of Central European pastry shops. Daddy attended auctions downtown, not to buy, just to look. But one day he returned proudly displaying a treasure: a Leica camera, which accompanied us on all our travels from then on.

Mother and Daddy sometimes left me alone when they went to the opera or to dinners with friends. On those evenings I was allowed to sleep in their bed, with a light on, until they returned; then my father carried me to my bed in the other room. One night, I woke up in their bed around two a.m., the light still on, my heart racing. *They're never coming back! What will I do now?* It was not until many years later, in therapy, that I made the connection between that fear and the time I had spent on the farm in the summer of 1944. The same sense of utter abandonment, the same panicked response. *If I don't get used to this, I'll die.* When my parents return a little while later, they find me sitting up in bed, wide-eyed. They hug me, kiss me, assure me they'll never leave me—this had simply been an extra late night, nothing for me to worry about. I believed them, but I may have concluded, then or later, that it's better to abandon people than to be abandoned—not a good recipe for intimate relations, I admit. But one does not choose one's deepest impulses.

On Sunday afternoons, we often went for walks around the city with other Hungarian refugees and their children. *Spazieren* in German, *sétálni* in Hungarian, walking with no destination— the French call it *flânerie*. I found it incredibly boring, trailing after the adults or walking in front of them with the other kids. The adults never seemed to be at a loss for conversation, talking animatedly while we kids mainly moped. When we reached the city center, where all the nice shops were, we revived and played a game I had never played before and have not since. In front of a store window, whoever cried "This one's mine" before the others became the owner of every item on display. We jostled each other to be first, especially for jewelry stores and fancy clothing boutiques. It's not clear what we thought we would do with all that grown-up finery, but the fantasy of luxury ownership evidently had an appeal in those days of statelessness.

I was happier on the Sundays when we left the city and headed for the Vienna Woods, or for the formal park in front of Schönbrunn Palace, which had belonged to the emperor. The park was crisscrossed by long straight alleys of trees and shrubs that had been clipped to form walls on both sides, so one almost had the feeling of being in an enclosed space. Neither fully outside nor fully in, those ambiguous alleys were like our lives. We strolled down them, sometimes racing to where one alley met another one just like it and turned a corner. I tried not to think about the future.

You leave people behind, but then they find you again, or you find them. A few months after we arrived in Vienna, I had the great joy of seeing Aunt Rózsi and Uncle Jancsi again. They had bought their way out of Hungary after their lumber business was taken over by the newly installed communist government. Earlier, Jancsi had actually spent time in jail; the newspapers called him "the Lumber King," a bad capitalist. The harshest years of the regime, under Mátyás Rákosi, had begun in earnest, and there would be no more amateurishness at the border: minefields had been installed. To leave Hungary on foot had become impossible and would not be possible again until years later, when the 1956 uprising created an opportunity for a few weeks; but Rákosi's government had allowed the Lumber King and his wife to take a plane, as long as they left everything behind and promised not to return. Jancsi and Rózsi had managed to take at least something with them nevertheless, they informed us with big smiles. They had each swallowed several large diamonds before getting on the plane. I tried to imagine what they would have to do to retrieve them—gross! But those diamonds gave them a good start, something to live on. I have no idea what we were living on— perhaps savings, or more likely, aid from the American Joint Distribution Committee, which was very active in helping Jewish refugees after the war. This is one of those gaps I will never fill in, except with conjectures.

Among my mother's photos, I found several of our outings to the Vienna Woods with Rózsi and Jancsi that year. Almost invariably, everyone in those pictures is smiling or laughing, as if they had not a care in the world. In one photo, Rózsi and Mother stand near each other, but with enough space between them for a man I don't recognize, who actually looks a bit anxious. I stand behind and above them, my back against a tree trunk—evidently, I had clambered on a branch to make myself taller, for I tower over them. Rózsi is wearing her leather trench coat from Budapest, with a silk scarf around her neck; Mother wears a wide wool coat with a belt. She looks young and beau-

tiful, her face framed by thick black hair that falls in gentle waves below her ears. My hair is still in braids, though without the rooster's crown.

Where exactly were we, on that clear fall day? Did the woods so close to the city remind us of our Sunday outings in the Buda hills? They remind me of them now. In one photo, I am alone by the tree of the previous picture, on the edge of a stream. The tree has several thick low branches, and it looks like I either am about to climb onto one or have tried to climb and fallen off, because I am laughing while looking at the camera: *See what a silly thing I did!* But I succeeded eventually, because the next photo has me sitting on a branch with my feet propped on another, looking quite smug. All the trees are bare; it must have been late October or early November.

My father appears in some of these photos. He had never joined us on our Sunday hikes in Buda, because Sunday was not a holiday for the Orthodox Community Bureau and he always had work to do, he said. But in Vienna we were marking time and he had no job to go to. Besides, he loved spending time with his sister Rózsi, who had doted on him ever since she was a little

girl. Although she was several years younger than he, I sometimes had the impression that she felt protective toward him,
as if she were the practical one while he remained the dreamy
yeshiva student of her childhood. He could be quite practical
too, as he had demonstrated during our months in hiding, but
in a curious way he depended on her; he could discuss problems
with her and be sure she understood, while he and Mother were
often at odds—or not even at odds but out of touch, since he
kept a lot of worries to himself for fear of setting off a storm of
anxiety. Mother could display admirable toughness and even
bravery, like the time she cooked for the German officers who
were occupying our kitchen in the winter of 1944, or the hours
we spent without my father in Kosice. But she was less good at
thinking calmly, weighing options—the family didn't call her
hysterical for nothing.

One picture shows Rózsi, Daddy, and me, sitting at a
wooden picnic table in the autumn sun, with glasses and bottles
before us—it may have been on the same day as the photos by
the tree. Daddy looks very handsome, in a tweed coat and stylish
fedora, leaning on an elbow and looking into the distance; on
the table in front of him is the leather case of the Leica. Maybe
he was trying out the camera, and that's why there are so many
photos of that day's outing. He had handed the camera to Jancsi
to take this one.

The last photo is from several months later and shows us
in heavy snow. This time Jancsi is in the picture, wearing a tall
black fur hat. Mother, her head in a kerchief, stands next to him,
dressed in a long skirt, heavy jacket, and hiking boots. Rózsi and
I are sitting on a sled in front of them, bundled in warm coats;
I lean back against her, and she has placed a protective hand on
my arm. Several skiers are visible in the background, emerging
from among snow-covered trees. As I examine the photo more
closely, I notice that Mother's stomach is bulging slightly. Could

she have been pregnant then? A few weeks later, she had to be rushed to the hospital, just like in the summer when my cousin Agnes and her family were visiting us from Paris. This was all a mystery to me, but I understood that despite their quarrels, Mother and Daddy were bonded in ways I could only guess at.

Their passions kept me busy as I tried to figure them out. While Mother was in the hospital, Daddy and I often went to visit another Hungarian refugee family—they too were a three-some, and the daughter was about my age. She was taller than I, and much prettier, I thought, with dark blond hair the same color as her mother's. Her mother was pretty too, and projected an air of calm self-confidence I found very appealing, prob-ably because calmness was not a trait I associated with my own mother. My friend and I play in one room while Daddy and the lady have tea in another; my friend's father is often absent. I am aware of the low hum of conversation and the occasional happy laugh in the other room, and it occurs to me to wonder why we visit them so often while Mother is away. After she returns from the hospital, I hear her screaming at Daddy one evening: "That blond whore! That blond whore!" We never saw that family again.

In the spring, anxiety set in. We couldn't stay in Vienna forever, but where could we go? This was the subject of endless discussions among the grown-ups. My parents wanted to go to America, but everyone wanted to go to America! One phrase they kept repeating was "DP camp in Salzburg." Should they apply to go to that camp? Could they reach America from there? Some people had been waiting for years, they had heard, and there was no guarantee you wouldn't be sent to Israel or Australia instead. What were DPs and DP camps, I wondered. Displaced persons, my father said. (Obviously, all this talk was in Hungarian—but somehow the phrase *DP camp* is in my memory in English, pronounced with a heavy Hungarian accent: *Dee-Pee kemp*.) Many thousands of Jews who had survived the Holocaust in concentration camps had no desire to return to their native country, and most of them were in the DP camps, my father explained. But we had been happy in Hungary, hadn't we? I asked. And we had never been to a concentration camp—were we displaced persons? Well, he said, we had had to hide from the Nazis and were persecuted during the war, so no wonder we had chosen to leave the country—that made us displaced persons. Yes, but didn't we do that to get away from the communists? That too, he replied.

In fact, the same questions tormented my parents as well. Did we really belong in a DP camp, with all those unfortunate people, most of them Yiddish-speaking, who had lost their whole families? We had lost many family members too, but our immediate loved ones had survived. We had even flourished in the years right after the war, so why call ourselves displaced persons?

But why not? We had left everything behind, hadn't we? Would we ever speak Hungarian again, except among ourselves? The discussions went on, with no decision in sight.

In the end it was Uncle Nick, the providential uncle who had arranged Granny's and Uncle Laci's departure from Budapest two years earlier, who decided for us. "Don't go to Salzburg," he wrote his sister and brother-in-law, "come to Haiti instead." He owned a shoe factory in Haiti, near Port-au-Prince, and he knew influential people who could help us. It would be easier to apply for entry to the United States from Port-au-Prince than to wait in line with all the other refugees in Salzburg; plus, Daddy's status as a rabbi gave him some precedence in the quota system. (U.S. immigration policy in the 1950s, with strict quotas based on country of origin, gave very little pride of place to Eastern Europeans.) Nick had given the same advice to their sister Magdi in Paris, and she and her family were already in Port-au-Prince—her husband worked with Nick at the factory. We should come too, he wrote. Unfortunately he could not help Daddy's sister, he added, but most likely she and her husband had their own contacts. He was right about that, for Rózsi and Jancsi had already left Vienna and would settle in Toronto a year later.

So there it was—we would soon be leaving on a long journey, to an exotic place. I was glad there was no more talk of DP camps. Just recently, a nephew sent me copies of two documents he had found by searching the digital archive of the American Joint Distribution Committee. They were both headed *Index Card AJDC Emigration Service Vienna*. The AJDC was in charge of Jewish displaced persons dossiers; one card bore the name *RUBIN Lilly*, the other *RUBIN Susanne*, me. Both declared the holder to be stateless, "formerly Hungarian," and both listed the country of destination as the USA. The dossiers were opened on October 10, 1949, and closed on June 14, 1950. Clearly, my parents had registered as DPs not long after we arrived in Vienna (why there is no card for my father is a mystery), but eight months later they abandoned their request.

The most exciting piece of news for me was that I would be reunited with my cousin Agnes, whom I had idolized two summers earlier. You lose people, but then you find them again. Would the magic between us still hold? The question never occurred to me—there could be no doubt about it. But what was life like in Port-au-Prince, I wondered. Were there many white people there? I had not seen people of color before, except for the waiter at the pool club where we went in the summer, who was very black and very handsome and wore a fez. He was from Africa, that was all we knew about him. Where in Africa was he from? How and when did he learn Hungarian, that impossible language? How long had he been living in the country? Nobody thought of asking him as he brought us our iced drinks and pastries. Now we would be going to a country where all the people were black, except for Uncle Nick and a few others. I wondered whether all the men wore a fez.

There were no kosher butchers in Haiti, we could be sure of that. My father therefore decided to learn the art of kosher slaughtering, and bought a gleaming set of tools for it. Actually, it was a single tool, a shiny instrument that looked like a large scalpel. It came in a velvet-lined case, along with a sharpening stone; the knife had to be razor sharp at all times, for according to Jewish law the putting to death of animals must be done with one swift stroke across the neck. That will empty the animal of its blood, which is forbidden for us to consume, and also guarantee the animal's quick and humane death, at least in principle. My father spent hours sharpening his razor-knife, then testing its sharpness on his thumbnail. I assume someone taught him how to do the killing, practicing on live chickens, but I never saw that part. I was quite fascinated by the gleaming knife and by the rituals that accompanied it. This must have been the kind of knife Abraham was ready to use on his son Isaac, on Mount Moriah. But my gentle daddy would never do such a thing to me!

Armed with my father's slaughtering knife and camera, and our traveling chess set, we were ready to leave Vienna. Now it was just a matter of waiting for the right documents. I didn't know what those were but trusted in the infallibility of Uncle Nick. In due time the documents arrived, and a concrete travel plan took shape. We would fly to Munich, our first plane ride! And from there to Paris, where we would stay for a week or two in Aunt Magdi and Uncle Béla's (and Agnes's) old apartment; they had left it to Uncle Béla's sister, another refugee, who had been living in Paris for a couple of years and would soon be leaving as well. While we were there she would go and stay with friends. Then we would take a train to Le Havre and sail on a big ship to the New World.

On a clear day in late May or early June 1950, we boarded our first airplane. The only thing I remember about that flight to Munich is that I was scared to death, and that I vomited into the bag the stewardess gave me when the plane started bucking. Back then, before jet engines, planes bucked often. I could not understand how the stewardesses, who were all young and slim and wore peaked hats as part of their uniform, managed to look so composed when I felt so miserable. And why on earth would anyone go up in a plane over and over, when they didn't have to? The ride was not very long, and I stumbled down the stairs to the tarmac gratefully. There would be another plane to take in a few hours, but I didn't want to think about that. I blocked it out so successfully that I have no memory at all of the next leg of the trip. Could it be that we didn't fly to Paris but took a train instead? Anything is possible.

I do recall that someone met us after that first flight and we sat with him in a cafeteria at the airport. I think Uncle Nick had sent him—in any case, he was from America. I don't recall what language we spoke with him, but it could not have been English—probably it was German, or maybe even Hungarian. The grown-ups order coffee, and for me he orders a drink he says I absolutely must try. "This is the most popular drink in America. You will love it." The drink is bubbly and black, and comes in an oddly shaped bottle that the waiter empties into a tall glass he hands to me with a straw. "Coca-Cola," the man says with a broad smile. "Taste it, it's delicious." I take a sip. It's sweet yet medicinal, foul-tasting. I have a hard time not spitting it out. "Well, how do you like it?" the man asks. I cannot bring myself to reply. "You have to get used to it," he says. "You'll see, you'll love it." I wonder whether I have failed an important test—was this a foretaste of what awaits me, once we finally reach America? If I have to learn to love this concoction Americans are crazy about, I will never become a real American! I have been an American now for close to seven decades, but confess that I have never learned to love Coke or Pepsi.

Baguettes, on the other hand, required no effort at all. From the moment we arrived in Paris, I was in love with the city and its bread. Using my best French, I ask the lady at the bakery for "*une baguette, s'il vous plaît*," which is often still warm when she hands it to me. I carry the long golden rod, wrapped around the middle in a thin strip of paper, as if it were a precious wand. By the time we reach our apartment, half of it has been eaten—not just by me, by all three of us. The combination of crusty exterior and chewy interior is irresistible, we all agree. *Vive la France!*

Our lodging was in St. Mandé, a crowded eastern suburb near the Bois de Vincennes. Today it is a fairly prosperous area (though not as prosperous as the western suburbs), but back then it struck us as poor. Aunt Magdi and her family had lived in a very small apartment with minimal comfort. (*"Apartment* is a glorified term for it," my cousin Agnes tells me. "It was three tiny adjacent rooms in a rooming house!") The toilet was in the hall, shared by all the tenants on the floor, and the combination kitchen-bathroom consisted of a hot plate and a sink—no tub, no shower. Many people in Paris during those years lived that way, not just people in rooming houses—they went to public baths, which were found all over the city, once a week and used the sink on the other days. It was hard to imagine that Agnes's family had lived that way for years, but we didn't really care about the amenities, for we spent most of our days outside. The weather was beautiful and we roamed the city like true tourists. We loved the Tuileries Gardens and the Grands Boulevards, with their huge department stores and movie houses that looked like palaces. Daddy took us to the Rex, the biggest cinema in Europe, with its glittering interior all in red plush and gold—I remember the excitement of the event, but not what film we saw there. (The Rex still stands, updated, on the Boulevard Poissonnière.)

One morning we dressed extra carefully, because later we were going to visit a distant cousin of my mother's who lived in the Hotel de la Paix on the Place de l'Opéra, above the famous Café de la Paix. We had never met anyone who lived in a hotel, and a luxurious one at that; we supposed he was very rich. Cousin Maurice received us cordially, in a large, beautifully furnished living room—the contrast between his abode and our place in St. Mandé could not have been more striking. He introduced us to his wife, a French lady who offered us drinks and a snack of thickly sliced cucumbers in sour cream that made us all sick afterward—we were used to cucumbers in the Hungarian style, sliced paper thin, doused with white vinegar and sprinkled with paprika; but we appreciated the gesture and thanked them profusely when we left. I had started to notice that refugees always had to be grateful for things; it made me uncomfortable, as if we were the eternal poor relations. If my parents were hoping for anything more from this rich cousin, they didn't say. In any case, we did not see him again.

On a particularly beautiful day we took the train to Versailles, so much bigger and more splendid than Schönbrünn Palace! Daddy put his Leica to use again, taking photos of Mother and me in front of an elaborate fountain and elsewhere on those grounds that dwarfed all visitors. I think my deep sense of attachment to France, especially to Paris, which I often think of as my second home, took root during those magical weeks of discovery. I had not yet fallen in love with French literature or with the figure of the intellectual, that very French creation (Émile Zola's screed "J'Accuse!" was legendary even in Hungary), but I already loved the tastes and sights of Paris. Even after all these years, I often catch my breath when I see Notre-Dame Cathedral in the distance while crossing a bridge, or watch children launch their boats in the fountain in the Luxembourg Gardens, next to parterres of flowers that change with the seasons.

Not all was perfect even in Paris. One morning, a few days after we arrived, we found ourselves in an office at the Préfecture de Police, a stone's throw from Notre-Dame. The building was imposing, but the office was like all government offices, cold and dismal-looking. We needed some kind of permit during our stay, probably because we didn't have proper passports. Two policemen interviewed us, and I felt very useful and important acting as interpreter. One of them proceeded to fill out an official-looking document, but when he handed it to my father, I saw Daddy turn pale, then purple with rage. Under the rubric of *race*, the policeman had written *Juive*, Jewish. "Jewishness is not a race, it's a religion," my father screamed. "How dare you, you filthy Nazi!" I did not need to translate that.

Strangely, I no longer recall how the story ended. Were we unceremoniously escorted out of the office, document in hand? Did the policeman cross out the word *Juive*? Did he at least answer my father? And what was *race* doing on that document in the first place? By 1950, surely official documents would no longer contain that holdover from Vichy—yet the memory is so vivid that I cannot possibly have imagined it. The vision of my father screaming with outrage retains all its sharpness. Evidently, "Jewish race" brought to his mind the humiliations and dangers of the Hitler years: the exclusions, the deportations, the Nazi craziness about "racial hygiene." I don't know how much he knew about France's collaboration with the Nazis, but he must have known enough. Under the Vichy régime, Jews in France, *la race juive*, had been deprived of their rights and many thousands were deported, despite the famous slogan of *Liberté, Égalité, Fraternité*. The French policeman's labeling of Jews as a "race" had unleashed a fury in my father that he may not even have realized he possessed.

I have never forgotten that scene, even if what immediately followed it is a blank. Many years later, in an essay I wrote about Jean-Paul Sartre's well-meaning book *Antisemite and Jew*, I took the author to task for his apparently unwitting use of antisemitic stereotypes, and especially for writing that he "would not deny that there exists a Jewish race." Really, he would not deny it? I fumed, outraged. Sartre was a longstanding hero of mine, and when I had first read that book I had admired his tour de force analysis of what motivates antisemites: insecurity and fear of the Other. Clearly, Sartre was not an antisemite. But upon rereading the section on Jews while preparing to write the essay, I felt almost betrayed. How could he accept the idea of a "Jewish race," especially after the horrors of the Holocaust? (*Antisemite and Jew* was published in 1946.) My father's enraged face at the

Préfecture de Police in the spring of 1950 must have hovered in the back of my mind as I wrote.

Sometime around the middle of June, we took a train to Le Havre. My father and I played chess with our clever little chess set, looking up from time to time to admire the countryside. Those carefully tended French fields, marked off by copses of trees and shrubbery, dotted with church steeples and occasional chateaus in the background, still enthrall me every time I watch them from a train window. It takes centuries of civilization to arrive at that degree of order. Back then, of course, I had no such thoughts, but chess too is a kind of order, and that may have been one reason why I cherished it. Despite all the pleasures of travel and tourism, ours was a disordered life, full of uncertainty and doubt about the future. Concentrating on the chess pieces, moving them according to their prescribed routes, kept the disorder at bay.

6

St. Christopher Medal

We bought the straw hats on a beach in Martinique, where the ship dropped anchor for a few hours and the passengers were ferried by dinghies to the beach, welcomed by strolling sellers of souvenirs and other must-have items for tourists. One merchant had a whole array of straw hats. After trying on all the possible models, Mother and I chose those with the broadest rims against the tropical sun. Then I and my new shipboard friend Danuta, a thin, blond Lithuanian girl who was traveling with her mother and grandmother, stripped to our bathing suits and ran toward the water. I waded in self-confidently, expecting to swim the way I had always done in the pool at the swimming club near Budapest, with my face down. When the first wave hit and filled my mouth with salt water, I came up sputtering, desperate to spit out the bitter taste. After that I was more careful, trying to keep my head above the water, but soon gave up and scurried back to the beach. The New World was not like the Old!

Of our trip across the Atlantic, a single photo remains. It shows a small group of adults and children, our shipboard community, standing in front of what looks like a wall, but it was actually the hull of the ocean liner. The photo was taken (by Daddy, as usual) at the end of our journey, after the ship had docked in Caracas. We are a ragtag bunch of Europeans, some already dressed for the tropics. Mother and two other young women wear light cotton dresses and sandals, and the straw hats from Martinique; Mother's is set at a slightly rakish angle, like that of a Cuban bandleader. Another woman, standing next to her husband, is still dressed in European style: narrow dark skirt, long-sleeved blouse, black pumps, and a white shawl draped over her head. I am standing next to Danuta, in front; we too wear cotton sundresses, with large round straw hats perched on our heads.

It was the end of June, hot and muggy. The group photo was our last show of solidarity, after we had exchanged addresses and many good wishes for the continuation of our journeys, knowing full well that it was unlikely we would ever meet again. (I did meet Danuta years later, when we were both in college on the East Coast, but since that fact and our earlier sea journey was all we had in common, we did not see each other again.) Mother, Daddy, and I then took a taxi to the airport and landed in Port-au-Prince a few hours later.

Everyone was there to greet us: Aunt Magdi, Uncle Béla, Agnes—and Uncle Nick, who turned out to be surprisingly young for a rich uncle and benefactor. He was thirty-six at the time, with a round face like that of all the Sterns and a head of curly brown hair. He embraced Mother heartily (the last time he had seen her, he was still a teenager), shook hands with Daddy, and held his arms out to me. I hugged him shyly—his face was smooth and smelled good. Then I turned and fell into Agnes's arms. She had grown into a young woman since our summer together, holding herself very straight, aware of her body in a new way. But I could tell she was happy to see me. "You'll see, it's terrific here," she said, linking my arm in hers as we walked toward the car. "We have a big house, there is a swim club even nicer than the one in Hungary. And we have a butler!"

That was my introduction to neocolonialism, 1950s style. Uncle Nick had rented a large house with a wide veranda that could accommodate all of us; it had separate rooms for Agnes and me and our parents, as well as for Nick and his companion, Martha, an American woman he had met not long before and whom he would soon marry. And yes, the house came with a butler and a cook, in addition to a laundress. The butler was a tall, dignified Black man dressed in white shirt and trousers, who served us cold drinks on the veranda whenever we called for them. His name was Preston, and Agnes and I called for him often—but he liked us because we spoke to him in French, and Agnes had even learned some words in Creole during the year she had already lived there. As for the cook, Françoise, she made excellent dinners that we all ate together in the dining room. Our kosher regime began the day after we arrived, when Daddy slaughtered his first chicken. After that he killed one or more each day, and we ate chicken in one form or another every evening.

We were often joined around the table by another Hungarian family Nick had taken under his wing. They were refugees with two young boys, whose mother bore a tattooed number on her arm. "She was in Auschwitz," my mother whispered to me more than once. I looked at that woman with awe, but she appeared to me just like other Europeans: about Mother's age, fortyish, medium build, dark haired. She often had a hard, anxious look on her face, but many refugees had that. Maybe she suffered from nightmares and woke up screaming in the middle of the night, when only her family could hear her. Still, I asked myself how she could look and act so normal, having survived a place whose very name evoked horror. *What happens to people who come out alive from hell*, I wondered. But I never dared to ask her about her time in the camp, and no one else did either. Right after the war, some camp survivors had published books about their experiences, and decades later thousands contributed their testimonies to video archives devoted to that purpose. But in 1950, wartime suffering was a taboo subject, even though all of us had stories to tell. Everyone was anxious to "turn the page," "put the past behind us," or whatever comforting cliché they could come up with in order to keep going, their eyes firmly fixed on what was ahead of them, never looking back. Psychologists tell us that trauma survivors often cope that way, pushing the traumatic experience into the background of their consciousness, where it can remain for a very long time. In the 1950s, the larger culture encouraged this kind of coping: after the first shock of discovery of the Nazi camps right after the war, the subject wouldn't come to the fore of public consciousness again until the Eichmann trial, in 1961.

Another frequent visitor to our house was a young man in his late twenties, with mischievous eyes, curly black hair, and a small mustache. Pista was the kid brother of Bözsike, the Auschwitz survivor, and he worked in some capacity for Uncle Nick—it was thanks to him that Bözsike and her family had landed in Haiti. Pista laughed a lot, and he was a very good dancer, Agnes told me. I could see that there was something between them, but she was only fifteen, I told myself. Still, it did not take her long to confide in me: she and Pista were in love and hoped to marry someday. In the months that followed, I became the keeper of all her secrets, happy to be her adoring sidekick again. (Agnes and Pista married a few years later, but the marriage did not last long.)

As in Vienna, but even more so, we were in Port-au-Prince without being part of it. We were not even part of the tiny Jewish community on the island, as far as I can recall. Jewish traders and businessmen had been coming to Haiti ever since colonial times; in the late 1930s, just before the outbreak of World War II, several hundred Jewish refugees from Austria and Germany had obtained visas from a benevolent consul in Hamburg, swelling the Jewish population on the island. (Most of them left in the late 1950s, but there is still a very small number of Jews in Port-au-Prince, according to some newspaper accounts written around the time of the earthquake of 2010, which brought Haiti into the spotlight of international attention.) Uncle Nick may have known some of those Jewish immigrants, but his ties were above all with the Haitian business community; he also knew, necessarily, the ins and outs of Haitian politics. He told us about the president who had been ousted just weeks before we arrived, a man named Estimé, and about the new man in power, Paul Magloire. Haiti had been the first colony to free itself from France more than a century earlier, and since then, it had had more kings and emperors and presidents than could be counted, he said with a laugh. Since the middle of the nineteenth century, the country was a republic and they were all presidents. Some lasted only a few weeks, others as long as ten years, but sooner or later they were all thrown out, often absconding with the national treasury as they left the country. But Haiti's politics meant little to us—we were still in transit, still waiting, still wondering about the future. Meanwhile, we tried to enjoy ourselves.

In those days, Port-au-Prince was a bustling, lively city, with too much poverty but none of the terror that Haiti became known for a few years later, when "Papa Doc" Duvalier took power. Although we spent most of our time at the house or at the swim club Agnes had raved about, we would sometimes go to the market in the center of the city, where fruits and vegetables were in abundance. Women with huge baskets on their heads brought them from farms, some many miles away, early in the morning—we could see them from the house, walking gracefully, balancing their heavy load. Agnes loved the mangoes they sold, large and juicy, with a very strong taste. To me they tasted strange and I struggled to like them—I was still nostalgic for the cherries and peaches and apricots I had adored back in Budapest. But I liked walking around the noisy, colorful market, hanging on to Agnes's hand while Pista walked on her other side. One day, we stopped at a vendor selling wooden handicrafts and I bought a mahogany box with a beautifully carved cover, the word *Haiti* blending into the design of fruits and flowers. The cover has gotten loose over the years, but I still use it as a box to store odds and ends, another of my relics.

As for the swim club, it was beautiful, just as Agnes had said, with a clean, sparkling pool and a large stone terrace where they served lunch. The club was open both to whites and to the Haitian elite. Haitian society, like all others, had a class system. Membership in the elite was determined not only by money but by skin color: the lighter one's skin, the higher one's prestige. That too was part of the colonial legacy.

In July, the heat became oppressive; we slept under mosquito nets and left the windows open at night, but we still had difficulty sleeping. The only solution was to leave the city. Uncle Nick rented another house, up in the hills of Kenscoff, a village not far from Port-au-Prince where the altitude made the temperature cooler. The house was a large stone house, big enough for all of us, including Pista and the family of the Auschwitz survivor. It had an enormous living room where we would congregate in the evening—the kids played board games or Ping-Pong while the adults chatted. During the day, we went walking in the hills, and Agnes and I even went horseback riding. I had never been on a horse, but they found me a gentle pony that was used to walking on those steep paths. One photo shows me and Agnes mounted on our steeds, wearing trousers and large straw hats. My pony is much smaller than her horse, and I am slouching while she sits tall

in her saddle. Don Quixote and Sancho Panza, setting out on their adventures.

Another photo shows all of us, adults and children (despite her secret romance, Agnes still counted as a child), squeezed close together on the veranda of the house in order to fit into the frame. Daddy is not in the picture—he was in the yard below, taking the photo with his Leica. In the center is Nick, the young master and host, flanked by his sister Magdi on one side and me on the other. Between Magdi and Mother is a visitor from New Rochelle, Cousin Harry, who had the prestige of being a citizen of the United States—maybe he was even born there. Nick himself had not obtained citizenship yet, so Harry was truly special, the only real American among us refugees. He looks just like the rest of the round-faced family, only a bit older; we would meet him again the following year, after we arrived in New York.

I turned eleven that month and we must have celebrated my birthday, even though I have no memory of it. The event that really stands out from our stay in Kenscoff was the slaughtering of the goat. After weeks of the nightly chicken, Daddy had decided we needed a change and arranged for a goat to be brought over from one of the neighboring farms. He would have preferred a lamb, but only goats were available. He had never killed a four-legged animal before, and there was considerable suspense and excitement over the project. Would he manage to do it with one swift stroke, as prescribed by the Law? I had never watched him kill the chickens, but this time I wanted to be there.

On the appointed morning, the animal arrived with the farmer. He held the poor thing down, while Daddy stood over it and swiped his knife across its neck. At that point I ran away and did not see what followed, but that night we had goat for dinner. I didn't like it; none of us did. Daddy went back to killing chickens.

After we returned to the city, it was time to think about school. The best school, we were told, was Sainte Rose de Lima, affectionately nicknamed Lalue, a boarding school run by French nuns that also took day students. Agnes had already attended it for a year before we arrived, and she vouched for the excellence of the teachers and the French curriculum. The best Haitian families sent their daughters there, and we would be among the few white students. In the beginning of September, wearing our uniforms of white blouse and navy blue skirt, Agnes and I set out for our first day of class. I was in fifth grade, she in the higher lycée.

The school occupied several buildings on lush, beautifully tended grounds, and from the moment I set foot in it I felt at home. Even more than in the French school in Vienna, here was a world of strict rules and ordered learning, where merit shone and hard work was duly rewarded. Every piece of homework was carefully graded on a scale of 1 to 20, *à la française*, with each error and the points it lost clearly marked in red pencil. Students were ranked in order of their grades, and the best ones received prizes at the end of the term. I sometimes wondered what the nuns thought of me, the little Jewish girl who strove so hard to be first in the class. Whatever they thought, they kept it to themselves, for they were scrupulous about treating every student equally. Since most of them were white, they may have had a special fondness for the few white students, but if so, they kept that hidden as well.

The nuns, from the order of St. Joseph, wore heavy long black habits and head coverings despite the tropical climate, and huge crucifixes hung on their chests. Beneath their imposing outfit they were kindly but unbending: notebooks had to be ruled just so, and every punctuation mark in a *dictée* had to be strictly observed. The *dictée* was a whole ceremony and continues thus in French schools to this day: the teacher reads a paragraph from a work of literature, word by word and sentence by sentence, pausing after every phrase to allow the students to catch up. Our job was to write down what she dictated. Her voice was calm, each syllable enunciated, every punctuation mark announced. Perfection in the recording was aimed for, but there was always the wrongly placed accent or the tricky verb ending to trip us up (*parlé*, *parler*, and *parlez* all sound the same), so perfection was almost never achieved. Still, it hovered on the horizon as our ideal. I loved it all.

The other activity I was introduced to in French class was diagramming sentences. You draw a straight horizontal line across the page, which is like the spinal cord holding subject-verb-object in place. Then you add the appendages—prepositions, adjectives, adverbs, relative clauses, dangling like arms and legs from the main body of the sentence. Every sentence had its own shape, and it all made sense: language, like arithmetic, was orderly, I noted with satisfaction. But those sentence diagrams were also strange and beautiful, like fantastical creatures made of words, with all their parts attached. Many years later, when I was teaching a graduate seminar on Proust, we amused ourselves by trying to diagram one of his endless sentences—we eventually gave up, because the appendages became impossibly complicated and ran off the page.

Best of all, during those months at Lalue, I learned to read for pleasure in French. In Budapest I had devoured books but had left them all behind, and Hungarian books were nonexistent elsewhere as far as I knew. Although my French had improved in Vienna, devouring books in that language was out of the question. In Port-au-Prince, my appetite was unleashed at last. Agnes gave me *The Iliad* in French as told to children, but the books I really thrilled to had kids as heroes. The school library was stocked with musty children's classics like the novels of the Comtesse de Ségur, whose didactic stories had been popular ever since the 1860s. The countess was a strict moralist. The naughty little heroine of *The Misfortunes of Sophie (Les malheurs de Sophie)* was always getting into scrapes and being punished—she once fell into a pond and was almost allowed to drown to teach her a lesson! The goody two-shoes of *The Good Children (Les bons enfants)*, on the other hand, received cookies and hot chocolate. Many years later, I wrote my first book about a literary genre that I called the ideological novel, which divided the world into positive and negative characters, depending on the ideas they espoused. I criticized that Manichean worldview in my book, but to my eleven-year-old self the strict division between good and bad felt just right.

My favorite child hero was the creation of another nineteenth-century writer, whose work is still read today. Hector Malot's *Nobody's Boy (Sans famille)* tells the story of a boy named Rémi, who grows up an orphan but has the good fortune to be adopted by a loving peasant woman and then by a kindly traveling organ grinder with a monkey. In the end, Rémi discovers that he is not an orphan after all but the son of a wealthy family in England. All's well in a world where homeless children can find a haven at last, in starched white shirts with lace collars for good measure.

Life in our communal Hungarian home was not as genteel as that of an English squire, but it was good enough. Between school and its rules, Agnes and her romance, Preston with his cold drinks, and the nightly chicken, I felt quite happy. But I knew we were still marking time—soon we would be leaving for America, the dreamed-of haven, maybe even before the end of the school year. I would have to learn yet another language, get used to another school, maybe more than one. I yearned for stability.

Instead, even more change was on the way, for it had become apparent that Mother was pregnant. This time, she had passed the three-month mark without a miscarriage—if all went well, I would finally have a little sister or brother in a few months. The prospect thrilled me, but it was one more element of uncertainty—what would we do with a little baby in America? I could tell that Mother too was apprehensive, as were the other grown-ups; this was not the ideal time to add a baby to the family. But Mother and Daddy had been trying and failing for so many years that the thought of a healthy delivery made everyone rejoice. Mother had just turned forty-two, way beyond the normal childbearing age among Europeans at that time; this was her last chance.

My sister was born in the beginning of December, at seven months, very prematurely—but she lived. There were no incubators in Haiti, so the doctors swaddled her in a thick layer of surgical cotton beneath her clothes; my parents prayed that the entry papers for the U.S. would arrive in time to get her to a hospital in America. They called her Eve Judith—"A little Évike, like our biblical foremother," Daddy said. She and Mother were now home from the hospital, and she remained alive. She had a dusky complexion and black hair, and tiny hands I never tired of examining; her fingers could already clasp mine. I still went to school every day, but my mind was on that little creature, so beautiful and so fragile.

About two weeks after she was born, the papers arrived. I announced to my teachers that we were leaving and I wouldn't be back the following term. They kissed me on both cheeks and gave me presents: fistfuls of colored pictures of saints and a medal of St. Christopher, patron saint of voyagers. These were my secret, for I knew Daddy would not be happy to see me treasuring Catholic trinkets. I got rid of the pictures on our way to New York but hung on to the medal, hiding it in my suitcase between two layers of clothes. What good ideas Catholics had, to turn to intercessors to keep them safe! I was not yet ready to ask what this thought implied about my own sense of who I was and where I belonged. For now, St. Christopher could watch over me.

A few days later, we carried baby Eve (we would soon be calling her Judy, Eve being just a flourish) onto the plane in a wicker basket, product of Haiti. Wrapped in her surgical cotton, covered with blankets, she slept through it all. A few hours later, we landed in Miami and took a taxi straight from the airport to Mount Sinai Hospital, where she was placed in an incubator. We visited her every day, watching her through the glass window. As soon as the doctors said she was ready to travel, we took another plane to New York, where Granny was waiting for us.

We were about to become Americans.

Part III
America

7

Green and White Chevrolet

"You must taste this," our hostess tells me, cradling a colorful cardboard box in her arm. "American kids love it. Look, it says 'Snap, crackle, pop' on the box, and it makes that sound when you pour the milk in." She says this last sentence in English, for Mother has bragged to her about how quickly I am learning the language.

We arrived in New York a few days ago and have come to pay a visit to somebody's relative. There will be many such visits over the coming weeks; it's the refugee thing to do. We have even learned a new word: *greenhorn.* The word has been around for hundreds of years, referring to young animals not yet savvy in the ways of the herd. Now it refers to new immigrants to America, people who need all the advice they can get. Today's advice-giver is an attractive Hungarian woman who has lived in New York for many years and is the owner of a successful business, a hair salon on Fifth Avenue. If anyone can give us tips on how to navigate our way in our new country, this well-coiffed lady surely can.

We sit on the sofa in her tastefully furnished living room, Mother holding the baby, as we face our hostess and her husband (also Hungarian) in armchairs. Feeling awkward, like poor relations again. She coos at the baby while her husband engages my father in talk about the New York subway system; then she turns her attention to me. "Come," she says, "I want to show you something." We walk into her kitchen and she sits me down at the breakfast table, then opens a cabinet and takes out the cardboard box. It's Sunday afternoon, way past breakfast time, but "it's never too late to eat cereal," she says, and I really must try this. She fills a bowl with what look like small pebbles, pours in some milk, then smiles: "Voilà! Give a taste." Suddenly, I remember the gentleman at the Munich airport who vaunted the merits of Coca-Cola. Will this new food wonder be another unpleasant surprise? But Rice Krispies turn out to be delicious, and the little pebbles really do make a crackling sound. Maybe becoming American will not be as difficult as I feared.

I cannot remember what it felt like to see Granny again. I was not the same little girl she had spoiled and coddled and fattened up with her noodle dishes—oh, those plump dumplings with a plum in the middle, those *palacsintas*, crêpes rolled up with homemade apricot jam! In Budapest I had basked in her adoration of me, her treating me like a precious child. Now I was a big sister, and as the only member of my family to have made quick progress in English, I was often called on to act as a simultaneous interpreter. Way beyond coddling. But she was still my familiar Granny, and I could tell by the way she looked at me that her love for me was as alive as ever.

Granny lived in a tall apartment building on York Avenue and 88th Street, near the mayor's mansion. It was a large brick box with low ceilings, an ugly piece of utilitarian modernism, but to us it looked like a sleek skyscraper. Granny's apartment was on an upper floor, with plenty of light; Uncle Nick was paying the rent. We were to stay with her until we found a place of our own, which all of us hoped would not take long, because there was only one bedroom and a pull-out sofa in the living room. The other major piece of furniture there was a brand new television set, the first one I had ever seen. Granny showed it off proudly and assured me I would love watching her favorite programs with her. She did not know more than a few words of English but felt quite at home with the latest gadgets in New York. In 1951, having a black-and-white TV in your home was not all that unusual, Google tells me, but still, only about half of U.S. households could boast that machine. Granny was in the avant-garde. In the months that fol-

lowed, she introduced me to Milton Berle, Jack Benny, Molly Goldberg (Yoo-hoo, Mrs. Goldberg—to think that she too was American!), and *Dragnet*. The stone-faced Jack Webb predictably requesting "Just the facts, ma'am" every Sunday night guaranteed that justice would prevail, as did the four dramatic notes that introduced each episode: *tam-da-dum-dom*, like the opening notes of Beethoven's Fifth Symphony.

Granny gave us the bedroom, and we squeezed into it with our suitcases. My parents slept in the bed, baby Judy in her basket, and I on a cot. Each night I could hear Mother and Daddy whispering long after we had gone to bed, she sounding more and more agitated as he tried to comfort her. Clearly, they were worried about our future. The Joint Distribution Commit-

tee supported new immigrants for a while, but my father had to look for a more permanent source of income. His rabbinical degree from a Hungarian yeshiva was of doubtful value on the Upper East Side of Manhattan, and the fact that he knew very little English was no help. Still, something would come up, he assured my mother—she shouldn't worry so much. But she had to buy clothes for the baby, she wailed, and where would we live after Granny's? I tossed and turned all night, wondering what would become of us.

Luckily, there was school. A few days after we arrived, my father took me to the public elementary school on 86th Street, where I was enrolled in sixth grade. I had learned some English during our two weeks in Miami, where I had discovered the wonder of comic books. For just a nickel or a dime you could buy one at the newsdealer, and I fell on them like a hungry dinner guest. Round-faced Little Lulu was my favorite, because the words were simple and the pictures helped to make out their meaning; soon I graduated to more advanced fare, the adventures of redheaded Archie and his friends. They had not exactly prepared me for sixth-grade English, but the good French nuns' grammar lessons stood me in good stead. I knew the parts of speech, and the diagrams we had drawn had taught me how sentences are put together. Now it was just a matter of transferring those skills onto English. Besides, I had no choice. The prevailing educational philosophy at the time was that foreign students must learn English quickly, with no coddling: sink or swim. I knew how to swim, even if the waters were choppy at first.

Math, at least, presented no difficulties. Numbers did not vary from country to country, and I was proud to get perfect scores on the weekly tests. But there too, no quarter was shown to foreigners. One day, my score was ruined because I had written the number 1 in the European style, with a little tail on top, which made it look like an American 7. The teacher, a woman with tightly curled blue-white hair that matched her icy persona, had read it as a 7 and had marked my answer wrong. When I tried to explain, showing her that my 7s had a little cross in the middle, in the European manner, which proved that the other was really a 1, her only reply was: "You're in America now." As she fully expected, I never wrote my 1s in the old way again, and also stopped crossing my 7s. If becoming American required giving up a few strokes of the pen, I was happy to make the sacrifice.

But what was I to begin with? A girl, a Jew, a Hungarian, a refugee. Zsuzsika in Budapest, Suzanne in Port-au-Prince, Susan in New York: no single label seemed to fit. I wanted to be American, yet I hated Coca-Cola, and hidden in my Jewish suitcase was a medal dedicated to a Catholic saint. Occasionally, I would take out the St. Chrisopher medal and hold it in my hand, remembering the classrooms at Lalue and the *dictées*, and wondering whether I would ever return to Haiti. Had the nuns been trying to tell me something when they gave me the medal?

Was it better to be a Christian, protected by many intercessors, than a Jew, facing danger alone? "The Lord is my shepherd"— it was a Jew who wrote that, but I did not feel very shepherded. Yes, we had survived and finally arrived in a safe harbor; but this was due more to luck and our own ingenuity than to divine intervention, I told myself, though not exactly in those words. I am fairly certain that already then I felt it was best to rely on oneself and one's family, not on supernatural forces, in times of crisis.

In that case, what was I doing with St. Christopher?

One evening, not long after we had arrived in New York, I found myself alone in Granny's bedroom, standing by the window with the medal in my hand. Suddenly, barely conscious of what I was doing, I pulled up the sash and flung the medal down into the street. I did not hear it land; it was too small and we were too far up. But I felt strangely elated, as if I had accomplished something important. My gesture had been impulsive, unpremeditated. Still, I had made a decision: I was not a Christian. I have not been an observant Jew or even a believer in God for many years, but my attachment to a certain Jewish identity—that of a "Godless Jew" who attends synagogue a couple of times a year, and who knows the melodies of all the prayers—has not wavered. (I also made sure that both of my sons had their bar mitzvahs. One is not the daughter of a rabbi for nothing.)

I looked out at the dark sky and closed the window.

The first years we spent in America are difficult to sort into specific dates. Some memories are clearly dated, marked by the school calendar or by summer vacations; others stand out just as sharply, but it's not clear exactly where they belong in time. They are like isolated clouds floating in an atmosphere marked only by a certain mood, a certain color in the air. If I had to put a label on it, I would call the mood anxiety; the color would be light brown, or a dull gray.

As if all the other changes to get used to were not enough, shortly after we arrived in New York I began to sprout breasts. It confused and upset me, especially as people on the street sometimes took me for baby Judy's mother when I was wheeling her carriage. "Can't you tell I'm just a kid!" I wanted to scream whenever an old lady stopped to take a peek and asked, "Is she yours?" It did not occur to me that most people don't look carefully, that they tend to think in categories: a young female wheeling a baby must be the mother. Instead of amusing me, or perhaps making me proud to be taken for a grown-up, their error made me feel ashamed. It must be my breasts, that's why they mistake me for a woman, I thought. But I did not want to be a woman yet! It was hard enough to be a sixth-grader struggling to write her 7s correctly.

Mother had found a store in the neighborhood that sold lingerie, and took me there to buy a bra. "Only eleven years, but need a brassiere," she told the saleslady in her broken English. "Not a problem, many girls her age need them," the saleslady replied soothingly. She must have sensed my shame, and maybe my anger too. I was often angry at my mother in those days. Why didn't she speak English, why did she send me out to walk the baby alone, why didn't she make me feel better about my body? I was too young and self-engrossed to understand that, like me, she was strugglling to adjust to our new life, without her sister, without the camaraderie of other refugees that had sustained her in Port-au-Prince or Vienna, and with a new baby to care for ("at my age," she must have thought). She, for her part, did not have the insight or the energy to take the measure of my unhappiness. As a result, we each fought our battles alone.

I cannot say exactly when I started going to the movies by

myself on Sunday afternoons. It seems odd now that my mother allowed that, but as I said, she had many other things to worry about. Maybe I did not even tell her where I was going. There was a row of cinemas along 86th Street, between Third Avenue and Lexington, each with just one screen, and they changed their program often. I loved those dark rooms lit up by images that transported me to another world. Virginia Mayo, the perky blond co-ed dancing on top of a car (it must have been *She's Working Her Way Through College*, released in 1952), embodied my idea of American beauty. Burt Lancaster, the bare-chested Crimson Pirate swinging on a rope as he leapt from his ship, beckoned me to heroism and romance. But I discovered one afternoon that the movies could also be a site of shame and re-vulsion, when a man with a raincoat over his arm sat down next to me. His presence so close to me made me feel uncomfortable, especially as there were empty rows all around us. Suddenly, I felt his hand creeping up my thigh under my skirt. I froze: the creep was molesting me! Could it be my fault? Maybe I attracted types like him. *Do I look like that kind of girl?* I finally got up and stumbled to a seat a few rows away; meanwhile, all the pleasure had disappeared, leaving only a bitter aftertaste.

Curiously enough, I kept going back to the movies. But from then on I was on the alert: the minute a raincoat sat down next to me, I would get up and move. None of them tried to follow me, but each time it happened, the thrill of the dark room disappeared. Sometimes no raincoats came, and those were perfect afternoons.

Daddy, meanwhile, was looking for solutions to our larger problems. After a few weeks (or maybe months—it's all a blur) of living with Granny, he found us an apartment nearby, on the corner of York Avenue and 83rd Street. This was no high-rise brick box but a traditional fourth-floor walk-up, with a front stoop and fire escapes. Our apartment was on the third floor, with all the rooms lined up in a row, railroad style. The rooms were small, but I was happy to have one to myself, its windows overlooking the street.

The neighborhood was full of Hungarian and Eastern European immigrants. Paprikas Weiss, a venerable grocery store that catered to Hungarians, was a few blocks from our house, on Second Avenue and 82nd Street; Mother went there to buy poppy seeds for her pastries. Small restaurants with Hungarian waiters lined Second Avenue, serving goulash and chicken paprikas among other dishes from the old country. Being kosher, we did not eat there, but I found one of those restaurants still thriving when I returned to the neighborhood many years later, this time to have a meal. There were also a few Hungarian clubs, some of which catered to Jewish refugees. A quite large number of non-Jewish Hungarians had fled the country with the German army when the Russians marched in, in January 1945. Many of these Hungarians were antisemites, a fact that created a chasm between the Jewish and non-Jewish refugees (who nevertheless shared many of the same tastes in food and music—one of the paradoxes of nationality in Central Europe). My uncle Laci often went to the Jewish Hungarian club, looking for old acquaintances or making new ones. My parents, however, had no desire to look back at the country they had left behind. Like me, they were eager to make their way in America.

We settled in to our new apartment, but Daddy still hadn't found a way to earn a living. He was in touch with some acquaintances in the Orthodox community in Brooklyn, who knew him from Budapest. They got him occasional gigs as a rabbi or *cohen* (various Jewish rituals require the presence of one or the other), but these were not regular enough, and his choosing not to live in Brooklyn added another obstacle. While most of the Orthodox refugees from Hungary had settled near each other in Borough Park (or if they were Hasidic, in Williamsburg), where they could reconstitute a communal life not unlike the one they had enjoyed in the old country, he had preferred Manhattan: one more sign of his divided self, but also of his striving. In Borough Park, one could get by speaking Yiddish or Hungarian almost all the time; where we lived, you had to know English, and he was doing his best to learn.

One day he remembered that his father had told him about a cousin who had emigrated to America many years earlier and had become very rich. His name was Joseph D., and he lived in New York. When my father looked him up, he realized that Cousin Joseph was indeed a very rich man, the head of a major real estate empire in the city. I remember going with Daddy to visit Joseph D. in his office, in midtown Manhattan. He was a small man, around sixty, sitting behind an immense desk; the glass wall in his office (also immense) offered stunning views of the sky and the skyline. Clearly, Mr. D. did not have much time for poor refugee relatives. But he did remember his cousin Yehoshuah Baruch from the old country. He told my father to think about what he might be able to do to earn a living, and to come see him again the following week.

After conferring with my mother, Daddy returned to Cousin Joseph's office and told him that his wife had been the co-owner of a kosher butcher store in Budapest after the war, so maybe he could open a shop here. She could not be the cashier, as she had been in Budapest, because of the baby, but she could advise him. Mr. D. nodded. Being a man of action, he did not linger or hesitate: "Good idea. I'll give you five thousand dollars to get you started," he told my father. "Go find a place, maybe in Queens." Five thousand dollars was a very considerable sum in 1951, equivalent to over fifty thousand in 2020. "But mind you," Joseph D. added, "This will be the only help I'll give you." Sink or swim.

My father, elated, set about finding a good location in Queens for a kosher butcher store. After a few weeks spent consulting with my mother and various people he knew, he decided on the relatively up-and-coming neighborhood of Kew Gardens, where a storefront was available on a commercial street near the subway. It was not a bad choice, for Orthodox Jews had started moving into the neighborhood just around that time. But the one thing he and Mother had not thought about was that in Budapest she had been partners with a man who knew about meat, a butcher. Daddy knew nothing about meat, even if he had slaughtered many chickens and even a goat in Haiti. Besides, as everyone said, his sister Rózsi was the one with a head for business, not he. It took less than a year for the store to go belly up. Cousin Joseph had said "sink or swim," and Daddy had sunk. There was no more help to be sought from him. I think my father was too ashamed to even inform him of his failure.

Mother had hysterics in the kitchen every night: she might as well commit suicide! One night I actually saw my father struggling with her to pry a large knife from her hand. I ran into my room, frightened but also furious: Had she forgotten that her husband had a serious heart condition? The doctors in Budapest had been adamant: too much excitement was bad for his heart, yet here she was having tantrums and threatening to kill herself every night. I dug into my schoolbooks to block out the feelings of rage and helplessness.

At least one thing remained after the wreck of the butcher shop: the slightly used Chevrolet my father had bought with some of Cousin Joseph's money for the daily commute to Kew Gardens. It was a two-tone sedan that I remember as green and white, though this is one of those details I may be inventing. The important fact is that it was our very first car (in Budapest, we had walked or taken public transportation), and that aside from its practical usefulness, it represented the promise of the New World. *See the USA, in your Chevrolet!* the TV blared each evening. Yes, we hoped we would.

As a start, we often drove out to New Rochelle with Granny on Sunday afternoons to visit her cousin Harry, the American who had spent time with us in Haiti the previous year. He and his wife, a tall dark-haired woman who favored long skirts and sandals, lived in a large house with a perfectly mowed front lawn and a landscaped backyard—it seemed to us the epitome of American success. They always received us warmly, offering tea and cakes, happy to show us the latest appliances in their well-equipped kitchen. When the weather was warm, we sat on lawn chairs in the backyard, admiring the neatly clipped shrubbery. Years afterward, when we were living in Chicago, my parents dreamed of owning a house like that and spent many Sunday afternoons attending open houses in the suburbs. That dream never came true, but back in New York in 1951, even the dream seemed out of reach. We were greenhorns, poor relations. In the car on the way home after those visits, I would see my mother's face darkening. That evening, there would surely be another scene of despair in our cramped apartment.

As had happened before, one of Mother's brothers came to the rescue. This time it was Uncle Laci, the resourceful one who had survived forced-labor camp in Hungary and had left the country with Granny in 1948. He had been away when we first arrived in New York, but we had often seen him since then. Laci had the reputation in the family of being a "bohemian," a lover of theater, art, cafés, and horse races. But he was also a shrewd businessman, and he had figured out a way to make a living without having to work too hard. He owned a stock of oil paintings, still lifes and landscapes as well as folkloric village scenes, that he commissioned from Hungarian artists in

Paris and New York, and he traveled the country by car with a young Hungarian man who acted as his driver, making stops in Cleveland, Chicago, and other big cities with Hungarian enclaves. His method was simple: upon arrival, he would look up doctors in the Yellow Pages and call those with Hungarian-sounding names, offering to show them original oil paintings by Hungarian artists, with no obligation to buy. His easygoing manner and smooth talking did the rest.

Many a living room of the prosperous medical establishment in the Midwest was filled with paintings sold to the lucky owner by Lester Stern, traveling art dealer. By the time we arrived in New York, he had a circle of customers he visited regularly. Laci was then forty-six years old and had gotten married only recently, to an American woman he had met two years earlier on a train to California. (It was a long trip.) His wife Lillian had been in the Women's Army Corps during the war, she told us proudly. After the war, she became a public school teacher in New York City. She and Laci had an affectionate, harmonious marriage that lasted until her death many years later, each one living an independent life in addition to the one they shared. Thanks to Lillian, Laci had gotten a green card, on the way to American citizenship, as had Granny.

Now he made my father an offer. Why not travel together on his next trip? He needed a driver, since he did not drive; Daddy could fill that role, and he would split the profits with him. He knew Daddy would have much better prospects eventually, he said, but in the meantime this could be a stopgap. My father accepted gratefully: he really would be seeing the USA in his Chevrolet! They made several trips together during our years in New York. I suspect Daddy was not unhappy to leave our anxious little family behind for a few weeks.

In the summer of 1951, my father was offered a job as the summer rabbi to a small Orthodox synagogue in the Catskills. The pay was minuscule and the job lasted only the season, but it came with a house that had a large backyard, perfect for the baby. We piled into our Chevrolet and moved up for two months to the sleepy village of Tannersville, about a hundred miles from New York City.

Today, Tannersville is a thriving resort and ski town, drawing tourists in both summer and winter, according to its visitors' bureau. In the nineteenth century, it had been renowned for its tanneries (as its name implies), but by the 1950s its industries had declined and tourism had not yet replaced them; there was very little going on in the town. But there was the Orthodox synagogue, Tannersville being a modest part of the Borscht Belt, a summer haven for Jews fleeing from the New York heat. It had no glittering resorts like Grossinger's or the Concord, but there were lakes for swimming and the mountain air was cool and clear. The outstanding feature of the town, as far as I was concerned, was its public library, a tiny, dusty wooden house with a sign outside the door and very few readers on the premises. I don't even recollect the presence of a librarian, although there must have been somebody in charge. It was there that I discovered the girl detective Nancy Drew, whose father was a successful lawyer and who had a handsome boyfriend, as well as the ever-clever Hardy Boys. I gobbled up the books in the two series, dreaming about American teenagers who lived in small towns where everybody knew them.

I did not know anybody in Tannersville, or anywhere else where real Americans lived. Still, it was a pleasant summer. We went swimming in a nearby lake every day, and I made friends with a girl from the synagogue, about my age, who often came over to play. We set up a croquet field in the backyard, or maybe it was the synagogue that had one in its yard—either way, we played a lot of croquet that summer and I read a lot of Nancy Drew books. The following year, Daddy was invited again and we returned to Tannersville for another stint—that time I discovered *Little Women* and its sequels, a definite step forward. Naturally, I identified with Jo, who possesses both brains and beauty. While not the prettiest of the March girls, she is the smartest, and most importantly, she is happy in love as well as work. Greta Gerwig's recent film version suggests that Alcott wanted to keep Jo unmarried but bowed to her publisher's pressure by having her marry the Professor. But I was like her publisher, conventional: I wanted Jo to be happily married, in addition to being the strong, independent, working woman that she was. Why shouldn't she have it all? I certainly hoped I would, even if I was not ready yet to put that hope into words.

In the fall of 1951, a whole new life started for me. The previous spring, we sixth-graders had undergone a large number of standardized tests. I had never seen a multiple-choice test but discovered soon enough that these were important, for they determined how we would be placed in junior high school. I warmed to the challenge and did very well, despite my halting knowledge of English. I was therefore assigned to a "7sp-9sp" class; *sp* stood for "special," which meant that the class would do three years' work in two. The junior high was an all-girls school on York Avenue and 81st Street, two blocks from where I lived. It had a large number of students, but our class kept to its own schedule and never mixed with the other girls—we were a selective school within the school, an elite, and proud of it. Quite striking, from today's perspective, was the racial and social diversity of that special class. There were several Puerto Rican girls, and one or two Black ones as well; more astonishingly, a few were white girls from wealthy families, who would almost never be found in a New York City public school today.

By miracle, I who had not had a close friend in school since Budapest became part of a small group, four girls who went through those two years as a close-knit unit. We even organized ourselves into a club and met once a week after school at the home of a girl named Caroline, who lived on Central Park West in a large apartment full of books and art works, with pale rugs on the polished floors. Caroline's mother was an art critic, her father a banker. Why their daughter went to school on York Avenue and 81st Street was a mystery to me, but I was very glad to spend time in their apartment, as were the other girls in our group, who like me lived in more modest lodgings. The group included a short, freckled red-haired girl named Joan, who was Jewish, and a tall Puerto Rican girl named Lila. We called ourselves the Rugbugs, inspired no doubt by the nubbly rugs we often sat on; it took several extended discussions to come up with that silly name, during which we consumed large quantities of cookies and juice served by the housekeeper. We never seemed to be at a loss of subjects to talk about, although I could not come up with a single one if I were asked to name one now. (I imagine boys must have been mentioned quite often, even if none of us came anywhere close to having a boyfriend.) Occasionally, Caroline's mother, an imposing woman with her hair pulled back into an elegant chignon, would come in and say hello. Otherwise, we were on our own, just how we wanted to be.

In fact, our group consisted of misfits. Caroline had a speech impediment, Lila was Puerto Rican, Joan was a Jew, and I was both a Jew and a foreigner. But New York was full of people like us; being misfits together suited us just fine. Of course, we did not put it that way to ourselves—that would have required an outsider's view, or a degree of self-knowledge few twelve-year-olds possess.

The teachers of our class were middle-aged white women, some of them extremely dedicated. The science teacher, my favorite, was famed for her no-nonsense attitude, and we all admired her because she taught us a lot and expected a lot in return. She looked austere, even stern, but she invited the girls who had gotten the highest grades on the weekly test to keep her company in her classroom at lunchtime, offering us her favorite crackers. I still think of her sometimes, all these years later, when I see boxes of Triscuits lined up in the cracker aisle of the supermarket. Like everything about her, her lunchtime offerings were precise and orderly: she would take three or four crackers out of the box and place them on a small paper plate, then hand us each a plate, this ritual being repeated from day to day. In her bearing and attitude, she probably came closest to the nuns I had found so reassuring at Lalue. We knew nothing about her personal life, other than that she was unmarried (she was "Miss") and totally devoted to her calling. Even though I don't remember what we talked about during those lunches, all of us felt it was a huge privilege to be near her. My love of science, which persisted right through my first years of college, started in that classroom, near the stern but kindly gray-haired woman who presided over it.

The English and social studies teacher, by contrast, had bleached blond hair that she often fussed with while she sat on a stool in front of the class, her plump legs crossed above the knee. She was "Mrs." She wore brightly colored dresses, had painted nails, and would spend a good part of the class period recounting anecdotes about her life. "She didn't prepare much for today," we exchanged mutely during some of her classes. Yet even she taught us something, and when she warmed to a subject she could become downright enticing. One day she spent the whole hour telling us about one of her favorite authors, a traveler and adventurer named Richard Halliburton who had written books with titles like *The Royal Road to Romance* and *The Glorious Adventure*. Most romantic of all, he had disappeared at sea before he turned forty, leaving behind a legend—like Amelia Earhart, she said. After that, I ran to the library to find books by Richard Halliburton. She was right, they were thrilling. I began to dream about meeting the author, who was very handsome according to the photo on the back flap; it never occurred to me that one day I might write books too, even if they were not as exciting as his. But I too yearned for adventure. Not the kind that was imposed on us, like the Christian masquerade during the war or the arrest at the border when we left Hungary, but the freely chosen adventure, the glorious one.

Not too many years later, in December 1960, that wish was gratified, in an incident that cured me of adventures for a while. I was spending a year after college studying in Paris, thanks to the combined generosity of my alma mater, Barnard, which had given me a small traveling scholarship, and the ever-benevolent Uncle Nick, whose graduation present consisted of a monthly check for one hundred dollars, delivered to me on the first of each month at his bank on the Place Vendôme. In those days, you could live on that sum in Paris if you had student housing and ate only in student restaurants, where the mediocrity of the food was offset by its costing almost nothing. One day at lunch, I made the acquaintance of two French students who were studying literature, Richard and Roger. Richard was the shorter one, good looking, with dark hair and dark eyes; Roger was fair, with a pleasant round face. He dragged one foot slightly, the result of polio he had contracted as a child. The two young men were big fans of André Malraux, who at that time was an aging politician, Charles de Gaulle's minister of culture, but who in the 1930s had been a dashing adventurer, an antifascist writer and public intellectual. He had traveled to Indochina as a young man and had written about Chinese revolutionaries, then fought against

Franco in the Spanish civil war, writing a great novel about that war. I had read a bit of Malraux in college, but Richard and Roger told me that the Spanish war novel *Man's Hope* was his masterpiece. I did not read it right away, but the idea of a writer who was also a man of action fighting for a good cause caught my imagination. A few years later, I would write my doctoral thesis on another writer of the 1930s, Paul Nizan, who had been an antifascist journalist as well as a novelist, and who had died tragically in World War II, while still a young man. (Clearly, my fascination with History's capital *H* goes back a long way).

In early December, Richard and Roger told me they were planning a ski trip to Austria and invited me to go with them. Roger had a friend in Vienna who knew of a mountain near the Italian border that had a hut on top; we would climb up to the hut on skis with a group of other students and stay there for a week after Christmas. I told them I had never skied before, but they said it wasn't hard to learn and there would be plenty of people to help me.

Uncle Nick, my benefactor, had invited me to meet him in Italy in early January, while he was there on a business trip. So I decided to combine the two trips, leaving for Milan straight from Austria after the skiing. A woman I knew in Paris lent me a ski outfit: pants, jacket, warm socks, and knitted hat and mittens. On the boys' advice, I bought a rucksack I would need for the hike up the mountain.

Did the prospect of being in Vienna again awake any nostalgia in me? I do not think so. The year we had spent there was long ago, and the circumstances were too different. Evidently, I was not yet ready to open up the memory door. We set out in high spirits on the day after Christmas, taking the overnight train to Vienna—no wagons-lits for us, just couchettes, berths where we slept with our clothes on, four to a cabin. Vienna, where we arrived in the early morning, was cold and snow-covered; we met Roger's Austrian friend (I will call him Werner), who introduced us to an American friend of his. The American, Robert, had never skied either, but he looked athletic and was eager for our mountain adventure. We spent the day outfitting ourselves with rented skis and boots—Werner volunteered to take mine back after our trip, as I would not be returning to Vienna.

Early the next morning, we took a train south to the small town of Klagenfurt. I had a suitcase with clothes for Italy but left it at the train station and stuffed the few clothes I would need during the week into my rucksack, along with a notebook in which I had been writing a diary throughout the fall. A bus took us to the base of the mountain, where we met up with the other members of our group—there were about ten of us, mostly boys, with one or two girls besides me. The Austrians were all expert skiers who knew the mountain well; they said it would take a few hours to get to the hut, but we should reach it well before nightfall. By then I was starting to feel uneasy, wondering whether I had been foolhardy to embark on this trip. Just carrying the skis and poles on my shoulder, balanced on my rucksack as Werner had taught me, had been a challenge. How would I feel once I had them on my feet?

One of the Austrians stayed behind to help Roger, Robert, and me, the least experienced members of the group. Richard went ahead with Werner and the others. Our guide showed Robert and me how to put the skis on; they were old-fashioned, made of wood, worn with hiking boots that fit into a springlike contraption—not quite cross-country skis, but closer to them than to the sleek downhill models I knew later. "Hold the pole like this, and dig it into the snow in front of you as you put your weight on the same foot," he instructed us. "You'll get the hang of it soon. But let's get started, we don't want to get caught in the dark."

Off we went, our leader in front and we three doing our best to follow. The snow on the trail was deep; putting one ski in front of the other while carrying the rucksack turned out to be less easy than it looked, especially since Werner had put a load of canned food into my rucksack just before we set out. "Everyone has to carry some of these," he said; "we'll have to do our own cooking at the hut." After an hour had passed I began to feel very tired and was tempted to stop and lie down in the snow. Robert and Roger were ahead of me but not by much. Our guide came skiing toward us, looking worried. "You really must try to go faster," he said. "We're way behind schedule and at this rate we won't reach the top before dark." He took my rucksack and added it to his own. No lying down in the snow now.

Finally, we reached the end of the wooded trail—but in front of us loomed an immense, steep slope. How would we get to the top? "You have to do the *steppentritt*—here, I'll show you," the Austrian said. The *steppentritt* was what we call the ladder step, an excruciatingly slow way to climb a mountain: you stand sideways to the slope, lift your right ski and move it up by a few inches, planting your right pole next to it, then bring the left ski up alongside—repeat as many times as it takes to get to the top. It takes thousands of steps, I discovered. The Austrian could do it like a dance, racing up the hill that way, but to the three of us it felt like an eternity. Even without my rucksack, I was out of breath, suffering from the cold despite all the physical effort. My hands felt frozen inside the mittens. And while we were climbing, inch by inch, it started to snow! The Austrian kept circling back, encouraging us, but there was nothing he could do to help. The snow was several feet deep, we could not take our skis off, we had to keep going. By then, as the darkness started to descend, I was telling myself that quite possibly I would die on that slope.

At last we arrived on the crest, in pitch dark. The snow was still falling, and our guide suddenly realized that he could not find the way to the hut—the snow had obliterated the tracks left by the earlier group. "We'll have to wait until morning," he said; "hopefully they'll send a search party for us." Meanwhile, the temperature had fallen even further and we were all shivering. We found a spot a few feet down that was slightly protected by a ledge and squeezed together underneath. We took our skis off and propped them against the ledge, creating a kind of enclosure. We opened the rucksacks and took out all the sweaters, as well as some dry food we could chew on. "We must try and make a fire," the Austrian said. He had some matches, but what could we burn? Roger spied the notebook in my rucksack and, grabbing it before I could stop him, started tearing out the pages. The Austrian struck a match, and I watched my diary go up in flames. I felt a helpless rage, watching the pages curl up and the writing disappear. Somewhere in that notebook was a sentence I was quite proud of, unaware that the French poet Mallarmé had said it much better decades before me: "Life has meaning only when it is written." Had the past few months suddenly been reduced to meaninglessness by these flames? I felt as if a part of me was burning; then I heard Roger say that it was more important to survive than to worry about a diary.

The fire didn't last long, but it helped a little. Afterward, we huddled together, seeking body warmth. "Don't sleep, you must keep awake!" the Austrian kept repeating. We slapped our hands together, tried breathing on them. There was no place to get up and walk, since we were sitting on a slope beneath that ledge. When the first light appeared, we struggled to stand and put on our skis. A few more *steppentritts* and we were back on the crest, looking for the way to the hut. Our guide seemed better oriented with the light, and we started on our trek—thank goodness, it was pretty flat up there, no more *steppentritts*. The sun was shining, its light bouncing in jeweled dots off the snow,

and if we had not been so dead tired and half in shock, we would
no doubt have stopped to admire it. After about half an hour, we
found our search party, or they found us. We followed them to
the hut, where we collapsed in relief.

During the week that followed, I almost never left the hut.
The others went out to ski every day; I stayed in and cooked.
The hut had minimal amenities, but it was well heated by the
woodstove we kept going night and day. We washed ourselves in
a basin of hot water when we could. I was mourning the loss of
my diary and dreading the day we would have to go back down
the mountain—how would I manage it? The thumb of my right
hand was turning black; it didn't hurt, but obviously something
was not right. I hoped it could wait until I reached Italy.

At the end of the week, we left the hut and somehow I
made my way down the slope that had almost killed me. In
Klagenfurt, I said goodbye to the others, collected my suitcase
in the station, and got on a train to Milan. Uncle Nick was
already there, staying at the luxurious Hotel Excelsior, which
seemed like the perfect antidote to the mountain. How I loved
the first hot bath I took there! After he saw my thumb, Nick
immediately arranged for an appointment with a doctor. It was
frostbite, the doctor told me—I was lucky the thumb didn't
have to be amputated. He gave me an injection and assured
me my thumb would return to normal in a few weeks. In the
meantime, I should go and enjoy the sights in Milan. Which
I did, followed by Florence (still with Uncle Nick) a few days
later. In Florence, I bought a dress of aquamarine blue wool. It
and Michelangelo's *David* became the highlights of that trip.

The next time I tried skiing was in 1969, in a resort in the
French Alps that had ski lifts and good hotel accommodations.
No more mountain huts for me.

In 1950s New York, adventures for twelve-year-olds were harder to come by. I did, however, have an adventure at school, mostly of the imposed kind. Because of our class's special status, we attracted the attention of other students, some of whom were what we called "fast girls"—they were older than us, many had boyfriends, and they hung around in groups on the sidewalk after school. Possibly because I still looked foreign, a few of them accosted me on York Avenue one afternoon in September, not long after the start of the school year, and demanded that I give them money. Their leader, who did the talking, was a tall, thin girl, almost scrawny, who chewed gum and wore a tight skirt with a slit up the side. She had a watchful, bitter expression that would have been striking even on a grown-up: it was as if life had already taught her some rough lessons and knocked her around. Strangely, the image that comes to my mind is Dorothea Lange's photo of the migrant mother, with her worn-out face and her skinniness. I had obviously never heard of Dorothea Lange then, and even now the association is odd because this girl appeared to me more dangerous than downtrodden. But she looked strangely dispossessed, despite her position of power in that group and over me. In retrospect, I feel a certain sympathy for her; back then, I felt simply frightened. I usually had a few coins on me, to buy treats at the candy store on the way home. I gave her the coins, then hurried home.

In the succeeding days, the same scene occurred several times, and I began to feel hunted. What to do? I finally decided to go and speak to the school principal. She listened to my story, then called in the assistant principal. I told her the story as well, and the three of us sat there for a while; then they said they needed to think about it and asked me to return the next day, before classes started. The next morning, it was the assistant principal who received me. She said they had decided I had grounds to bring a formal complaint against the girls, which would involve a hearing before a judge. Was I willing to testify in court about their bullying? I said yes. She said she approved of my decision—it was the right thing to do. And I shouldn't worry, she added: the school would make sure the girls didn't bother me again before the court hearing.

Looking back on it now, I can only wonder what made me say yes, without hesitation, to her question about testifying in court. Was it the kindly air of the assistant principal, or my trust in America, or simply a naïve desire to see justice done? I have often found myself, since then, in situations where more prudent souls would retreat or at least hesitate before forging ahead. This has earned me, among some of my friends, a reputation for fearlessness, but it could also be called a reckless foolhardiness (like agreeing to climb a mountain on skis when I had never skied before). A few years ago, the outspoken Hungarian philosopher Agnes Heller, who had survived the siege of Budapest as a teenager, wearing the yellow star, told me that after that experience, nothing could frighten her. Possibly, my episodes of recklessness have a similar origin: survivor's chutzpah. It must have occurred to me that the girls could attack me and hurt me, but I evidently felt protected by the law. I wonder whether such trust would be possible today. It's true that kids back then did not take guns to school, even if some beat up or bullied those they considered weak. Still, I must conclude that, not for the first time in my life, I was simply lucky.

Strangest of all, I cannot remember involving my parents in this affair. Is that a memory lapse, or did I truly exclude them? Did I tell myself that they could not help me and I had to deal with this by myself? Whatever the case, I am certain that on the appointed day it was just the assistant principal and I who took a taxi from the school to the courthouse, where we found the accused girls already waiting. I don't recall whether they were accompanied by adults, but probably they were. It was evidently a juvenile court, and no one had been arrested or jailed. A man who looked like a judge sat on the podium and asked me to tell the story yet again. I did, and pointed out the thin girl who had been the ringleader. Afterward, the assistant principal and I took a taxi back to school, and she congratulated me once more for having done the right thing. I continued with the remaining classes of the day as usual.

The fast girls were strictly admonished to keep away from me, and they did. A week or so later, after school, I bumped into the thin girl on York Avenue. My first impulse was to turn around, or else go past her without speaking, but she came toward me with a nonthreatening air. "The Yankees are winning!" she exclaimed happily. I knew nothing about baseball, but I knew it was the World Series, with the two New York teams facing off. "Great! What's the score?" I responded. She told me, and we both smiled happily and went our separate ways. I felt I had achieved a small step toward becoming American.

This whole story appears so bizarre to me today that I could almost imagine I dreamed it. But it was real. I have looked up the World Series for 1951: the Yankees played the Giants that year and won the series. It was Joe DiMaggio's last season with the team, and with baseball.

I have very few photos from those first years in New York. No doubt Daddy was too busy trying to figure out how to live to use his Leica much. But there are a few from the summer of 1951 in Tannersville, showing me and my new friend in our bathing suits, two pudgy preadolescent girls, shoulders bent, uncomfortable in their bodies. There is also a photo from earlier that spring, one of the rare ones I have of Granny in America. It shows the three of us: baby Judy, me, and Granny, who is holding the baby in her lap. Judy could not be more than five or six months old, and

Granny grips her firmly under the arm as she stands her up on her knee. Judy looks like a happy baby, dressed in a white sweater and matching overalls, her eyes shining and already intelligent. Granny looks at her tenderly while I sit at her side, on the edge of a hammock.

The photo was taken in the backyard of Cousin Harry's house in New Rochelle, on one of our visits that spring; Granny evidently got dressed up for the occasion. She wears a flowered dress with a pattern of large white daisies on a black background, quite attractive; around her neck is a gold chain, and pearl earrings dangle from her ears. Her left hand, gripping the baby, is covered with age spots, but it is manicured; on her ring finger she wears her wedding band and another ring, a pretty gold bow with a small diamond in the middle. She looks old (she was seventy-three at the time), but her skin is surprisingly smooth and her brow free of the horizontal lines I so dislike on mine. If Botox had existed in those days, one might almost think she had had a treatment. All in all, this was a woman who maintained her dignity, even in a foreign country whose language she would never master. As for me, I smile at the camera, with my usual round face and shoulder-length hair neatly combed. I wear a plaid skirt and a white short-sleeved blouse, beneath which the faint outline of a small brassiere is visible.

Trying to situate all this in a larger picture of 1951, I realize how oblivious we greenhorns were. Ethel and Julius Rosenberg were executed that June, the Korean War was raging, Joseph McCarthy's hunt for communists reached its height, and in a few months the World War II hero Dwight Eisenhower would be elected president. Historic events were all around us, but we were not involved. In a way, we were still just visitors in America.

In school, at least, I felt I belonged; there I was not a greenhorn but a member of "7sp-9sp," special in the good sense. When our second year started, in the fall of 1952, we were told that all of us should aspire to be admitted to one of the city's elite high schools. Hunter High and the Bronx High School of Science were at the top of the list, requiring a competitive entrance exam for admission. We spent most of the year preparing for the exam, and no one was more committed to seeing us succeed than our math teacher. She was a nervous, birdlike woman who held special sessions after school as the date of the exam approached. We crammed and crammed, for "failure is not an option," our sparrowy teacher kept repeating. I took the exam and was admitted to both schools, which made me very proud but also presented me with a difficult choice. In the end, possibly because of our science teacher's influence, I chose the Bronx High School of Science. Several other girls also decided to go there. The future looked exciting.

Then, one afternoon around the beginning of June, my father told me we would be leaving New York. His various attempts to earn a living having come to naught, he had enlisted a distant relative in Chicago to help him find a position—anywhere in the

United States would be fine, just so it paid a fixed salary. The relative, who had close connections with the Jewish community in the city, had found a job that my father must take, he said. It might not be exactly what he wanted, but as a start for a new immigrant, it was a good position. What was it? my father asked. *Shammes* at a large Conservative synagogue on the North Side, the relative replied. A *shammes*, or sexton, is a glorified building manager: he makes sure that all the prayer books are lined up before a service, that there are plenty of yarmulkes to go around, that the building is properly cleaned and maintained by the custodians. He may also help in the running of the service, calling people up to recite the blessings over the Torah; but it is a low-level position, and my father, who always put *Rabbi* before his name and prided himself on his reputation as a brilliant Talmudist, thought of it as downright humiliating. Yes, the relative told him, but he had no choice. Once he got settled and had learned English well enough, he could aspire to something higher—in the meantime, he should accept the offer. Swallowing his pride, my father did. The job was to start in the fall, just before the High Holidays.

I was devastated. To have worked so hard and have succeeded so well, only to have it all snatched away at the last minute! To leave my friends the Rugbugs, and Granny and Uncle Laci, to start over yet again in a strange city, in a strange school where nobody knows me. It's all terribly unfair, and there is nothing I can do about it. I promise to write regularly to Caroline, Joan, and Lila, and say tearful goodbyes. A few weeks later, Mother, Daddy, little Judy (a toddler by then), and I climb into the Chevrolet and leave New York behind. My dream of seeing the USA in our Chevrolet had been like a promise of freedom, but this feels more like imprisonment.

There was one small piece of consolation: during our two and a half years in New York, I had lost my foreign accent.

8

Seventeen

"Sue Rubin?"

"That's me."

The geometry teacher lifts a sheet from the stack on his desk, walks over to mine, and hands it to me: "Congratulations! You got a perfect score on Friday's test." The other students have all turned toward me, as if they had just realized I exist. They mostly ignored me during the first week of school, happily greeting each other after the summer vacation, while I wandered the hallways looking for my classroom or turned round and round in the immense cafeteria, holding my tray and wondering where I might sit. Now, suddenly, I have become visible. My face turns red; I feel vindicated.

After class, I am in the bathroom and a girl comes over to me as I stand by the sink. "Congratulations on the test," she says with a smile. "How are you?" Happy but flustered, I say brightly: "The brain is fine." I mean it to be funny, a bit of clever repartee. But she raises her eyebrow: "The brain?" She repeats the word with a touch of irony. I blush a deep purple. How could I have said that? Maybe she thinks I referred to myself as "the Brain," in the third person, as if I were royalty! A weirdo, this new girl. Before I can try to right the mistake (but how would I even start?), she has turned and left the bathroom.

This school stinks! I will never feel at home here.

Nicolas Senn High School, where I would spend the next three years, occupied a large city block surrounded by green spaces. It was an imposing building, with Greek columns at the entrance and a student population of three thousand, including a large Jewish contingent. Not a single student of color, as I recall. (Today, I learn from my internet search, the student body has shrunk to fifteen hundred, two-thirds of them African American or Hispanic and only 11 percent white, the result of Chicago's changing demographics and white flight to the suburbs.) During my first weeks there, despite my small triumph on the geometry test, I still had trouble every day deciding where to sit in the cafeteria at lunchtime, and when I finally sat down at a table with others, I was tongue-tied. Most of the students knew each other from freshman year, some as far back as kindergarten, while I was a sophomore who knew nobody, and even if I no longer had a foreign accent, I still lacked the ability to make small talk, to approach a group and introduce myself. I felt like an oddity and was sure everyone else saw me that way.

One day in the cafeteria I met a girl who was also new to the school, having recently moved to the neighborhood from the South Side. She told me there were different "cliques," and it mattered which clique you hooked up with. The Jewish kids belonged to various cliques, she explained, and much depended on the clothes you wore. She wore soft, oversize cashmere sweaters in beige or gray—that was a good thing to wear, she said. Later, I told my mother about this conversation and explained what a cashmere sweater was. She nodded.

Since I did not own any cashmere sweaters, I fell back on my usual solution: get good grades, be one of the smart kids. But I was sure I would never make friends. At the end of each day, I walk to the streetcar by myself and go home, feeling angry and depressed. In my room, I plunge into homework as into a pool. Just keep plowing ahead and don't think about the next three years.

One afternoon when I got home, I found three brightly colored sweaters spread out on my bed. "They're cashmere," Mother said proudly. She had found them on sale and bought them for me, expecting a joyful response. I was touched but realized right away that these sweaters would not get me into any cliques. They were lightweight and fit too tightly, not at all like the thick, luxurious pullovers in pale colors that the "in" kids wore. I did not have the heart to tell this to my mother, and pretended to be happy with her gift. I wore the sweaters to school, knowing full well that I was still an outsider.

Meanwhile, I was mourning my New York friends and the Bronx High School of Science. I wrote to Caroline, Joan, and Lila and they replied, but after a few months our correspondence faded. I cannot say who stopped writing first, but it may well have been me. Having left so many things behind during the preceding years, I had learned to draw a line over the past, allowing people as well as things to fade away. By now, I hardly even remembered the nuns of Port-au-Prince, who had made such a deep impression on me at the time; as for my classmates in Budapest or Vienna, they had receded to a shuttered room in my mind that I never visited. In films, an image will dissolve by becoming fainter and fainter. To me, only members of my family remained vivid: Cousin Agnes, Aunt Magdi, Aunt Rózsi, Uncle Nick, Uncle Laci, Granny. We had news of them, we hoped to see them again soon. Everyone else faded away. I am always full of wonder when someone mentions a friend they have known since elementary school. After I left Chicago, Senn High School dissolved as well. But for now, Chicago was my home and Senn was where I would spend a large part of every day. I had better make my peace with it if I wanted to survive.

Agudas Achim, the synagogue where my father worked, no longer exists. It was converted into an apartment building around 2018, its proud façade now the entrance to midpriced studio and one-bedroom rentals. I found pictures of the building online, taken by a photographer when it had already been abandoned but before the demolition started. Despite the graffiti that covered some of its walls, the sanctuary retained its aura: the huge two-story space could hold more than two thousand worshippers. Multiple arched stained-glass windows graced its walls, and elaborate mosaics framed the Torah ark.

In 1953, Agudas Achim was one of Chicago's premier synagogues, its architecture in the grand eclectic style. The façade boasted three arched entrances framed by fluted columns, and tall windows framed by more columns; it could have been a church, were it not for the two round openings, like portholes, filled by large Stars of David, and the small but unmistakable tablets of the Ten Commandments above the tall central window. This was clearly a Jewish building, proud to stake its claim in the city. Founded decades earlier by immigrants from Hungary, the synagogue was a flourishing enterprise, supported by the movement of Jews from the South Side of Chicago to the growing area in the north, near Lake Michigan.

My father found a welcoming community, although the title of *shammes* still stung him and would continue to do so for as long as he worked there. My sister was enrolled in the nursery school, and Mother soon made friends with one or two of the other mothers. The synagogue had found us a roomy apartment on Kenmore Avenue, a short walk away— that was necessary, since we did not ride on the Sabbath.

All in all, there was little to complain about. We were getting settled, Daddy had a steady job and had enrolled in night school to obtain a diploma (in what subject, I do not know, but there is a photo of him wearing a graduation outfit). He and Mother still spoke English with a heavy accent, stumbling over irregular verbs and the present perfect tense. But our family was making its way in the new country.

Sometime during that first semester at Senn, I became friendly with a girl who struck me as a perfect American. By a miracle I could hardly believe, she seemed genuinely interested in me. Her name was Nancy. She was tall and slender, with light brown hair she wore in a ponytail or else falling loose to her shoulders, and she had a self-possessed air I very much admired. I could not imagine her ever having doubts about her life.

Nancy lived with her parents in a three-story house with many rooms, and often invited me to visit her after school; her mother offered us home-baked cookies. A pleasant-looking middle-aged woman, Nancy's mom appeared to me calm and well organized, the exact opposite of my excitable mother, who could never keep her house in order. Nancy's house was always perfectly neat; the living room had an antique-looking sofa covered in velvet, dark wooden end tables, and upholstered armchairs you could sink into. When I thought of our cheap furniture, transported all the way from New York—Formica tables, wrought-iron lamps with ugly sausage-shaped shades —I felt ashamed. I never invited Nancy over, where she could have seen our house and met my mother.

In December, Nancy's family set up a huge Christmas tree in their living room. Her older brother, a sophomore at Oberlin, came home for the holidays, and there was much joy and excitement in the air as the family crowded around him. I was invited to a few of their parties, and kept hoping that the curly-haired boy who was Nancy's brother would take one look at me and fall in love, the way people did in the movies; but he never noticed me. Often, everyone would gather around the piano to sing carols while he played. I knew the words to many of the songs from school and joined in, but of course it was not the same. I had long ago decided that Christianity was not for me, yet Nancy and her family elicited my deepest longings—not as Christians but as Americans. They seemed so *normal*—that's what I was longing for, to be simply an American like everyone else. Of course, if I had not been so self-absorbed, I would have realized that many Americans were not simple in the way I dreamed of; even Nancy's family may have had immigrant grandparents from Germany or Ireland, but I never thought to ask about that.

In the spring, Nancy dropped me just as suddenly as she had chosen me. There was no fight or open break; she just stopped inviting me to her house after school and merely nodded when I passed her in the hall. I did not know why she no longer wanted to have anything to do with me, just as I had never understood why she had befriended me to begin with. But I still felt the sting of rejection, with its accompanying sadness and anger. Clearly, I had failed some unnamed test. It was a verdict all the more terrible for not being pronounced, only acted on.

If you don't want me, I'll do without you! I started going to the public library after school, to a branch not far from my house. I roam the open shelves, picking up books and reading the first page to see whether it appeals to me. For a while, I am fascinated by Queen Elizabeth, the Virgin Queen, and her unrequited love for Essex; later, I latch on to Abraham Lincoln and the Civil War when I read *John Brown's Body*, a gripping

book-length poem by an author I have never heard of, Stephen
Vincent Benét. Benét was a Pulitzer Prize–winning poet who
had died young of a heart attack a decade earlier, leaving behind
a long list of published works, but I discovered him the way I
did all the others, purely by chance. After Benét I found the
autobiography of Lincoln Steffens, a muckraking journalist I
admired because he wanted to change the world. It was a totally
undisciplined way of reading, stumbling from book to book.
Still, I found comfort in those forays into other lives, those rows
of orderly shelves that contained so much knowledge. During
that difficult time, the library was, as other libraries would be
again, my shelter from the storm.

I could not say the same about my home. My gradual
alienation from my mother now took an accelerated turn. I was
critical of everything she did, from child-rearing to the way she
behaved with my father; they still bickered almost daily, despite
their deeper understandings. I had a whole list of grievances
against her: she didn't read, she made me babysit for hours while
she went shopping, she didn't keep the house neat, she often
yelled. Gone were our happy outings in Budapest or Vienna.
In my eyes, Mother and I were enemies. "Boys don't like girls
who read too much," she would say, when I refused to put
down my book to set the table or take my sister for a walk.
"Besides, reading doesn't give you enough exercise and you're
getting fat," she would add. And topping it all off, "Your hair
is a mess. We have to find you a good place for a haircut." She
was right, my hair was a mess and I was getting fat, which made
me feel even worse about myself. But the reason I was fat was
not that I read too much, it was that I ate too much. I ate too
much for the same reason I read: to fill the void. I think what I
really held against my mother was that she could not help me
navigate the storms of adolescence. My storms were exacerbated
by all the baggage of my childhood—the war, the emigration,

the multiple displacements—but in some ways they were just ordinary teenage dramas that my parents were not well enough equipped to handle.

It took many years, all the way to my marriage and motherhood, for things to be all right again between Mother and me. The intimacy with her that I had felt in my childhood was gone forever, but we could bond over my sons, whom she adored; and she had always approved of my husband, who put on the charm for her. During my adolescence, I thought of her as narrow-minded, unintelligent even. But that was unjust. She was not an intellectual, had no desire to analyze her actions or gain insight into them, as the therapeutic jargon goes. But she was smart and plucky and had survived horrible losses by never looking back. When she was fifteen, her father died of a brain hemorrhage, leaving a large family with few resources. She and her younger sister were beautiful girls without a dowry, not a situation with brilliant marriage prospects in those days. No wonder she worried about my hair! But she was also ambitious for me, proud of my successes in school. She wanted me to be first in the class, even while she warned me not to read too much because boys don't like that.

In fact, with all her contradictions, she wanted for me all the things I wanted for myself— above all, in those years, assimilation to America. Unfortunately for our relationship, I had concluded that being American meant not being like her.

My relations with my father were also becoming difficult, though in a different way. I had always admired him, idolized him even, but now I began to challenge and provoke him. "If a shopkeeper strictly observes the Sabbath but cheats on his customers during the week, is he a good Jew?" I would launch at him on a Saturday afternoon. Or "What's better, to be an

atheist who helps people or an observant Jew who does not?"
He would look at me, surprised and then irritated. "You really
don't know what you're talking about," he would say, refusing
to engage in discussion. He was a brilliant Talmudist, but
that was a different kind of argumentation, and maybe, I
sometimes thought, he did not want to argue with a girl, even
if she was his daughter. We no longer played chess together,
and my exchanges with him were few, limited to banalities.
I knew that his job at the synagogue was frustrating to him,
since he felt he knew more than the American rabbi, yet he
had to keep quiet if he wanted to hold on to his job. It was not
a subject he could talk about with me, however.

Mother and Judy and I would attend services at the synagogue on the holidays, dressed up for the occasion as is the
custom; my father left the house before us so he could be there
at the beginning of the service, and when we arrived he would
gesture us to seats in the sanctuary. It was a beautiful space, and
the choir sang well. But I knew he disapproved of the choir, an
American invention—synagogues should not imitate churches,
he felt. He was a traditionalist when it came to Jewish practice
and theology, a *yeshiva bocher* from the old country, even if he
dressed in modern clothes. He would probably have been happier in an Orthodox synagogue, where women sat separately
from men.

During our time in Vienna, he had had an eye for beautiful
women, causing some tantrums by my mother. But he had aged
in America and put on extra pounds. Still a handsome man and
young enough in years (he was forty-three when we arrived in
Chicago), he no longer had either the energy or the lightness of
heart to engage in extramarital flirtations. He spent his Sabbath
afternoons studying the Talmud.

As for me, I began to grumble about Orthodoxy. Why
couldn't we go anywhere on Saturday, except maybe for a walk?

Some of the girls I knew at school met for lunch in a coffee shop and ate hamburgers with milkshakes. Why did I have to keep kosher? After a while, I no longer asked questions but did as I pleased, feeling guilty all the while—it is not easy to defy your father, especially if you love him. Mother knew about my transgressions, or at least suspected them, but did not tell Daddy.

The girl I sometimes met for a hamburger on Saturday (I still could not bring myself to order a milkshake to go with it: never mix meat with milk, says the Jewish law) was a friend I had made at school after Nancy dropped me. Beth was Jewish, a quiet, intelligent girl who was in many of my classes. She was an only child but not particularly close to her parents. Her father was a doctor, a small man who rarely spoke to us; her mother seemed to me nice but uninteresting, like the house they lived in, a nondescript ranch house with a smooth front lawn like all the others on the block. Most of my Jewish classmates lived in houses, not apartments—it was part of their upward mobility, along with their families' non-observance of Jewish dietary laws.

I liked Beth's calm manner, her even temper, and felt grateful not to be intimidated by her as I had been with Nancy. I enjoyed her company but did not long to be like her. She sometimes invited me to her house for a sleepover (an American custom that was new to me) and we exchanged confidences, though I did not tell her about my conflicts with my parents. Shame, ambivalence, despair were not the right subjects for midnight tête-à-têtes in a teenager's bedroom, I must have felt, amid the gingham throw pillows and the plush animals left over from an earlier time. The teddy bears I had had as a child were long gone, left behind with the red bicycle and the hills of Buda.

One bright spot during that unhappy time was that school gradually became a haven, just as it had been in New York. I reconnected with French, which I had neglected since leaving Haiti. I still loved science, especially chemistry, which was taught in a large room full of lab equipment: Bunsen burners, flasks and beakers of various sizes, cylinders, funnels, pipettes, each with its specific use, in an orderly universe presided over by the periodic table of the elements. My favorite courses, however, were in English. One year we studied Romantic poetry and Victorian novels, and I kept reciting to myself lines from Shelley's *Ode to the West Wind*: "Oh! lift me as a wave, a leaf, a cloud! I fall upon the thorns of life! I bleed!" Shelley was not a girl, and he was much wilder than I would ever dare to be, but I understood him perfectly. Thackeray, on the other hand, was a sardonic observer of life. *Vanity Fair* seemed endless in its catalog of human folly (also quite boring when Becky Sharp was not around), but I was delighted with its disenchanted final paragraph, which I committed to memory. "Ah! *Vanitas Vanitatum!* Which of us is happy in this world? Which of us has his desire? or, having it, is satisfied?" After that, as a last blow, Thackeray compares the characters we have been following for hundreds of pages to the puppets in a puppet play! Looking back on it, *Vanity Fair* seems like an unusual choice for a high school English class, but I felt I had scaled a mountain when I reached the last page.

I joined the school newspaper and loved the camaraderie that developed among us as we put each issue to bed every week. By senior year I had become news editor, writing a weekly column. I had quite forgotten about it until someone from Chicago that I met recently and who turned out to have been a classmate of mine at Senn sent me a copy of the *Senn News* from 1956, found in his mother's attic. There on page two of the April 13 issue was my photo, smiling, with very short hair and one of those white organdy collars that girls used to insert into a round-necked pullover. My column was titled "Potpourri" and was devoted mostly to announcements about upcoming Open House days by local colleges and universities. It also announced that eight creative writing students from Senn, including Susan

Rubin, had written poetry that had been accepted for publication by the *Annual Anthology of High School Poetry*. That I wrote poetry in those days is another fact I had forgotten.

The column was signed *Sue*. The years in Chicago were the only time in my life when I referred to myself by that abbreviated name. But I notice I was not consistent about it, for in the paragraph about the poetry winners I list my name as Susan. This was not the only doubleness I lived with during those years.

Around 1955, I started subscribing to *Seventeen* magazine. It was my family's only magazine subscription, and I paid for it from my earnings as a babysitter—another American invention I marveled at. To think that couples would go out every Saturday night, paying a teenage girl to stay in their home while the children slept! And they even invited me to raid their pantry. I did a lot of that, guiltily, hating myself for not being able to control my raging appetite. Whole boxes of cookies and crackers disappeared in one evening. The guilt increased even more when I sat down to read my copy of *Seventeen*, for all the girls in its pages had figures less full than mine. The magazine is still around, still advising teenage girls on how to dress, how to date, and what to hope for in life. Recently, some readers demanded that it stop airbrushing the photos of its models, allowing for variety in the shapes and sizes of teenage girls. But back in the 1950s there was just one model, and I aspired to it with all my heart. *Seventeen* was my bible of Americanness.

I recently read an article about the magazine's first years and learned that it was founded in 1944, targeted at thirteen- to nineteen-year-old high school girls. Its creators imagined the magazine's ideal reader, "Teena," as follows (this is from a piece of advertising copy): *Teena is 16 years old, 5 feet 4 inches tall, 118 pounds, attends public high school, expects to go to college—and then marry and stay home. Dad is a businessman/white collar worker and her family is middle class. She works after school hours (often babysitting) to make extra spending money.* I was the right height but several pounds heavier, and my Jewish immigrant family was not exactly the middle class that Teena's creators had in mind. On the whole, though, the copywriters had aimed true: *Our girl Teena wants to look, act and be just like the girl next door. She and her teen-mates speak the same language . . . wear the same clothes . . . eat the same foods . . . use the same brand of lipstick . . . For Teena and her teen-mates come in bunches—like bananas.* That comparison hurts, even retroactively! But I was not privy to the view of me that the magazine peddled to its advertisers. To them, Teena was a new female consumer and a marketing device; to me, she was the ideal American teenage girl, a model to emulate. (Needless to say, Teena was white.)

My parents too were aspiring to Americanness, or some version of it. They now spoke only English with my sister, whose knowledge of Hungarian consequently consists of no more than a few words. When they were alone with me, we often spoke Hungarian, but it was no longer the everyday language in our house. The bookshelves in our living room began to fill up with Reader's Digest Condensed Books, hardbound volumes that arrived four times a year. Each volume contained five bestsellers reduced to size, designed for the busy reader who just wanted the gist. I have looked up the volumes for those years. Most of the authors are forgotten, but some names still resonate: Herman Wouk, Alan Paton, A. J. Cronin, Pearl Buck, James Michener, John Hersey, the so-called middlebrow famous writers of the day. In truth, I never saw either Mother or Daddy reading those books. I think they planned to read them, however, like many other American book buyers with good intentions.

More importantly, my father had undertaken steps to leave behind the synagogue job that rankled him so much. One document my sister and I found after Mother died was an elaborately calligraphed text in Hebrew, which now hangs on the wall in my sister's house in Connecticut. It has been there for many years, but only recently have I realized exactly what it is. It is a *smicha*, an ordination certificate attesting to my father's training as a rabbi. Presumably, he had been given a similar document upon completing his yeshiva studies in Hungary, but he no longer had it. The Orthodox rabbis in Brooklyn who had gotten him summer jobs in the Catskills knew him from Budapest and required no document about his qualifications. But Chicago was different: if he wanted to be recognized as a man of learning, he would need to prove it.

According to this *smicha*, which a friend translated for me, two Orthodox rabbis in Chicago testified that they "found him to be a person who is filled with the blessing of God in Talmudic learning and biblical interpretation and in the intricacies of Torah, *halacha* [Jewish law], and all of the rulings that are derived from it." They also stated that "he is deserving of the post of a devoted rabbi in the community of Israel."

I fantasize about the exam he took to obtain this certificate: the rabbis as jury, seated, and my gray-haired father standing before them as they discuss intricate points in a Talmudic text. Maybe he gives a disquisition on Maimonides, like the one at his dinner of thanksgiving in Budapest. Reading the *smicha*'s flowery language full of superlatives, I can imagine how much satisfaction my father derived from this document, which confirmed that he really did know more than the Conservative rabbi who was his boss!

The Hebrew date on the *smicha* corresponds to April 25, 1955. It must have been around this time that my father obtained a teaching post at the Central Hebrew Day School, an Orthodox school for girls; he became the school's executive director a couple of years later. At that point, he could tell himself with some pride that he had attained success in America.

In the summer of 1955, possibly flush from my father's triumph with the *smicha*, we made an extended visit to our family in Canada. It was not our first summer car trip up north, nor the last, but it's the one that stands out in my memory because of all the photos that have survived from it.

Our first stop was Toronto, where Aunt Rózsi and her family had settled. Their numbers had increased since our days in Vienna, for Rózsi and Jancsi now had two children—their daughter Vivian was a year younger than my sister Judy (who was four and half that summer), and her brother Bobby was a baby. Uncle Jancsi's mother had joined them recently from Budapest and was living with them, in a house that also served as the office for their fledgling lumber business. Between the phones ringing and the children squealing and running around, it was chaos in the house, but a pleasant chaos. I loved being with Aunt Rózsi and Uncle Jancsi again and speaking only Hungarian—it was almost like being back in Budapest. Rózsi's older sister, Aunt Hera, who had left for Palestine in the 1930s, had arrived in Toronto the year before, with her husband and two sons. They too had lived in the house in the beginning but had found a place of their own since then. Hera had given birth to a daughter in December 1954, just a day after Rózsi's baby boy was born. The family was expanding, and I could barely keep track. The Israeli cousins knew no Hungarian, but Aunt Hera did—she was a warm and loving woman, a voracious reader, and I wished I had met her earlier. As it was, my heart belonged to her sister, whom I had loved since our motorcycling days in Budapest.

We stayed with them for a week or so, then headed east

to Montreal to visit Aunt Magdi and her family. Cousin Agnes had married Pista, her love from Haiti, the previous year, despite her parents' misgivings—she was only nineteen at the time. Pista's sister, the Auschwitz survivor, also lived in Montreal now, with her husband and two boys. It was a Port-au-Prince reunion, minus Uncle Nick. Aunt Magdi's sister-in-law, Uncle Béla's sister, who had taken over their Paris apartment when they left for Haiti, had ended up in Montreal as well, part of that small Hungarian-speaking colony. Margaret, or Manyi as she was called, had lived through the war in Istanbul and founded her own business. We heard stories about a great love affair that had ended badly; that plus the fact that she spoke Turkish in addition to Hungarian, English, French, and German, gave her a worldly aura I admired.

After a few days in Montreal, we moved to a village in the Laurentian mountains, about an hour's drive from the city, where my father had found his usual summer job as rabbi to an Orthodox congregation. The village was on a lake where we swam daily, and across the lake was a restaurant with a large deck where a jazz band played every night. Teenage vacationers gathered there to dance—it's where I learned to do the jitterbug. We all spoke French, another throwback to Port-au-Prince. It was a happy time.

Agnes, being a married woman now and working full time in Montreal, was no longer part of those joyful gatherings. I noted with regret that her marriage had created a distance between us, one that we never completely breached in the years to come. (As it turned out, her parents' qualms were justified, for she and Pista divorced very soon after emigrating to the United States. She met her second husband, an American, soon after, and they have been happily married for more than sixty years.)

Daddy made ample use of his Leica that summer, for the first time in a while. One photo shows Judy and Vivian, dark-haired little girls in matching bathing suits, sitting on twin chairs, or maybe rocks, in identical poses with big smiles on their face, in what looks like a country setting: scrubby grass, a dirt road. In another, Judy is shown alone in the same setting; behind her a wooden bungalow is visible, the kind one often finds for rent by the week in lakeside villages. On the back of both photos, in my father's careful handwriting, is the notation *Summer 1955.*

Where exactly were those pictures taken? It was clearly not Toronto, despite Vivian's presence. Once again, the shortcomings of my memory, so sharp about some things and so vague about others, are confirmed. It's from my cousin Agnes that I learn the necessary details. Vivian was with us in the Laurentian village—we had taken her along from Toronto as a playmate for Judy. Her parents must have been happy to have her out of the house for a few weeks, so it was a good arrangement for everyone. We dropped her off at home on our way back to the States.

The village being so close to Montreal, Aunt Magdi's family often joined us for the weekend. Uncle Béla, Magdi's husband, loved to fish for trout in the rivers nearby, wading into the water up to his knees. My father was definitely not a fisherman, but he liked to accompany him; I went along, and sometimes Béla's sister Manyi came too. On the days we went fishing, we would leave the house early in the morning, carrying a lunch of salami (kosher, for my father's sake), onions, hard-boiled eggs, and black bread, which Béla said reminded him of his childhood in Transylvania. For himself, he would often add a few slices of bacon. Once we got to the river, we would start the ritual of bait and hook, about which Béla was the expert. We would dutifully follow his instructions and wade into the water with him to cast our hooks as he showed us, but none of us ever caught a fish! After a couple of hours we would sit down for our country lunch, Béla cutting the slices of bread and the raw

onions with his pocket knife. As we chomped away, he would assure us that next time we would surely have better luck with the fish, but we didn't really care. The enjoyment was in the doing, not in the result.

One of these outings was immortalized by Daddy's Leica. The photo, evidently taken by Béla, shows Daddy standing behind a car with Illinois license plates (*Land of Lincoln*), biting into a hard-boiled egg. He is wearing shorts, leather sandals with closed toes, a short-sleeved white shirt, and a baseball cap turned backward. He cuts a strange figure, a middle-aged, somewhat paunchy man with thin, shapely legs, seen in half profile, his mouth wide open, his eyes turned sideways toward the camera. I don't remember ever seeing him in a baseball cap, but pictures don't lie; he must have worn it in place of a yarmulke. Next to

him, leaning against the back of the car, is Béla's sister Manyi, her hands in her pockets, looking as if she has seen many things in her life and nothing more could surprise her. The car is parked next to a body of water (not the river, more like a lake) and its doors are open, with two fishing rods propped against the back fender. A female figure stands in front of the car, looking down at something, her face partly hidden by the open door; she wears a kerchief on her head like a peasant woman in the old country. I recognize myself.

None of us looks as if they belong there. But I may be imagining that.

After that break from Americanness, we returned to Chicago and I resumed my project of becoming a teenager worthy of *Seventeen* magazine. It was the last year of high school, I had just turned sixteen, and I was determined. I lost weight, joined more clubs, wrote my column in the *Senn News* and signed it

Sue; in the spring, I was elected to the National Honor Society. I was also secretary and treasurer of the French club, secretary of the science fair club, and treasurer of the national journalism honors society Quill and Scroll, as well as its division president.

I know all this because I found the 1956 Senn yearbook online, a treasure for my challenged memory. (The actual yearbook, which I must have owned back then, disappeared in one of my many moves over the following decades.) My graduation photo shows a smiling girl who looks younger than many of her classmates, wearing a white pullover with an organdy collar tucked around her neck; she has a stylish haircut framing her face, with short bangs and a thin headband. Her name is Susan Madeline Rubin, nickname "Susie." That is one I have not seen anywhere but on that page.

I can also be found in several group photos in the yearbook, featuring individual clubs or activities. The most notable of these are the photos for Senn Hostesses, which get a double-page spread under the title *Guiding Stars of Senn*. The text below explains: *Whenever you see girls conducting visitors around Senn, look for the green badge that is the sign of SENN SENIOR HOST-ESS.* Senior girls with good grades could apply for membership in this honor club: *The members select new girls on the basis of activities, scholastic ratings, and teachers' recommendations.* Did I really need one more honor club enough to go to the trouble of applying for admission? Apparently, my thirst for recognition knew no bounds.

One of the Senior Hostesses' jobs, the yearbook informs me, "which always proves to be fun is trimming the Christmas tree." Sure enough, there is a photo of a large, beautifully deco-rated tree with three girls placing ornaments on it. I am not in that photo but in the one below it, which shows me standing with a tray of pastries in my hand, facing a girl who is holding plates. Behind us are two other girls, standing at a table with a pretty white cloth, laden with goodies. Clearly, this was the

party that followed the trimming of the tree. The captions list our names, most of which sound Jewish. My Jewish classmates, born and raised in America, were apparently also eager to join the majority culture—I doubt that the school had a ceremony for lighting the Chanukah menorah in December. This was Christmas 1955, when some of the Chicago suburbs still had covenants that forbade selling homes to Jews (as well as to Black people, of course).

I had failed the test in my short-lived friendship with Nancy two years earlier, but this was clearly a new page. I look quite slender in my white sweater (cashmere, I suppose), wear bobby socks and a full skirt that reaches almost to my ankles, and hold a tray of pastries at the annual Christmas party. How much more American can a girl get?

Only one thing was missing from this perfect picture: the

boyfriend. On the staff of *Senn News* I had several friends who were boys and would have been glad to partner up with one or two of them. But I was shy about making the first move, terrified of rejection, and I had never learned the art of letting a boy know you are available without having to say so. But that is not entirely true. I had never learned it properly, and my occasional clumsy attempts to send out signals usually met with failure and embarrassment. You can lead a horse to water, but you cannot make him drink; none of the boys I was interested in were thirsty when I was around.

Still, I managed to find a date for the senior prom—in those days, girls simply could not go to the prom alone. He was a boy I hardly knew, tall and somewhat awkward, with thick glasses. We were in some classes together and he often took the same streetcar that I did after school; one afternoon, a few weeks before the prom, he asked me to go with him. It was a date of convenience, based purely on the fact that we both wanted to be there—afterward, we never went on a date again. But on the night of the prom, he arrived at my house in his rented tuxedo, bearing a white gardenia to place around my wrist, as was the custom. I wore a strapless dress, like all the other girls. I cannot say that I was fully happy, but at least I appeared so.

Going through some papers recently that I had carefully set aside years ago but rarely consulted, I found the official document that had sealed my hard-earned Americanness: a certificate of naturalization issued in Chicago on June 5, 1956, by the Northern District Court of Illinois. The certificate, printed on cream-colored parchment, states that the court, having found that Susan Madeline Rubin had complied with all the applicable provisions of naturalization laws and "was certified to be admitted to citizenship, thereupon ordered that such person be and s/he was admitted as a citizen of the United States of America." The grammar seems a bit shaky, and I had to reread the sentence several times before it made sense. But the words are less important than the symbolic signifiance of that piece of parchment. In June 1956, a month before my seventeenth birthday and around the same time as my graduation from high school, I became a citizen of the United States and could claim all the privileges that went with that status. My signatures, in the middle of the document and beneath my passport-size photo imprinted with a large circular seal, confirm that I am indeed the person on whom that privilege has been conferred. My hair in the photo is not as stylishly cut as in the yearbook picture, but the face is definitely mine, with its wide-set brown eyes and full lips, on which there plays the slight shadow of a smile.

Given my overwhelming drive to conform to local norms, I wonder what made me look to Eastern schools for college. Most of my classmates thought of the University of Illinois at Urbana-Champaign, "downstate," as their default option: not quite a safety school, for it was selective, but anyone from Illinois with decent grades could count on being accepted there. Those with higher ambitions were eyeing Northwestern, the University of Chicago, or the University of Michigan at Ann Arbor, which had a special prestige; it was also quite far away, appealing to those who wanted to leave home. Very few were thinking of going farther east than that. Yet here I was, dreaming of Cornell University. I knew almost nothing about Cornell, and in those days nobody did campus visits before applying for admission (my parents could not have afforded visits anyway). But I liked the sound of the name *Cornell*. I knew the university had a high reputation, and the idea of a bucolic campus in a small town appealed to me. I could see myself walking with friends among green fields toward an ivy-covered building, talking about philosophy. I even wrote a story that semester in my creative writing class about a girl who has a similar dream but then discovers on her first day on campus that nobody around her wants to talk about philosophy! My sense of ironic deflation was already quite pronounced, it would appear. Or maybe the story simply expressed my anxiety: Despite all the honor clubs I belonged to, would I ever be qualified to talk about philosophy? Either way, the story marked me as off-center. I was not yet acquainted with Tonio Kröger, Thomas Mann's dark-haired dreamer who yearns (at least sometimes) to be like the blond, unthinking people he admires and at the same time scorns. But evidently, I too felt ambivalent toward the object of my desire. I was not the perfect specimen of "Teena" as described by the editors of *Seventeen* magazine, for she would never have written a story like that. Maybe more like a solitary mango than a banana in a bunch.

In the end, I applied to Michigan, Cornell, and Barnard College in New York City, as well as "downstate" for safety. Why Barnard and not Radcliffe, Bryn Mawr, or Smith? My decisions were made on impulse or based on hearsay, with no solid ground beneath them. But I knew what I did not want, even if I never said it in so many words, not even to myself. Since I had done well on the College Boards (as usual, I realized the importance of the multiple-choice exams), a number of local universities had sent me letters in the fall, inviting me to apply. I threw them all away, including the one from the University of Chicago, an outstanding university that offered me an attractive scholarship in addition. Clearly, I did not want to stay home, did not want to remain near the friends I had worked so hard to acquire. Only one other classmate was going east, a boy from the school paper who had been admitted to Harvard.

All of the colleges I applied to accepted me, but Cornell did not offer a scholarship, and that was crucial. Barnard offered a generous one—six hundred dollars per year, enough to cover the cost of tuition. It still required an equal amount from my parents for room and board, while Illinois would cost us nothing at all. But Barnard was one of the Seven Sisters, the girls' wing of the Ivy League, and it was part of Columbia, a great university. My parents were willing to take on the expense, even though it was a hardship for the family; we agreed that I would work every summer as my contribution. One afternoon, soon after I had accepted the offer from Barnard, my father took me aside. "Always remember this: It's better to be a small fish in a big pond than a big fish in a small pond," he said with great seriousness. I took that to be his blessing, a modest one to be sure. The third alternative, big fish in a big pond, did not occur to him.

Over the summer, my father spent several Sundays teaching me to drive. In the morning, before the crowds came, we would go to an empty parking lot and change places in the car. Sitting in the passenger seat, he would patiently guide me as I took my turn at the wheel. The car was automatic, not hard to learn. But he showed me how to brake gradually, not jam my foot down when I wanted to stop, and how to turn the wheel in one smooth motion, not jerkily. "Always keep your eyes on the road in front of you, but use your mirrors to see what's happening around you," he said. That seemed like good advice for more than driving. Those lessons brought back some of our earlier intimacy. Once again, he appeared to me as the loving, gentle father I had adored as a child. He was proud when I passed my driving test on the first try, despite my clumsiness at parallel parking. It would just take practice, he said.

Whether because of my rediscovered love for him or because I was leaving soon and suspected great changes ahead, that summer I started to observe the Sabbath again. I stopped going on Saturday lunch dates, ate only kosher meat, and generally did my best to live up to my father's expectations. He was pleased, I knew, but was there a genuine desire for religion behind my return to the fold? I don't recall ever asking myself that question. If I had, I would probably have had to admit that I lacked any real belief in God and was practicing a purely formal observance with no substance behind it. Or maybe the substance was simply a desire to affiliate—with my father, with Jewish traditions, with my and my family's history. And maybe at that time it was enough.

The other "enormous change at the last minute" (to quote the magnificent Grace Paley) was that I who had never had a boyfriend suddenly acquired two suitors that summer. Suitors is the right word, for they both declared their marital intentions. Jonathan was the older brother of one of my Senn classmates, an intense young man whom I met at a graduation party for his sister. He had just finished college, where he had studied philosophy, and he told me he wanted to start a dairy farm in the Illinois countryside in order to be close to nature. We spent long afternoons in his room, talking about this project and listening to records. He had studied the cello in high school and was especially fond of Brahms's double concerto for violin and cello, with its gorgeous melancholic melody. We would play the record over and over while he told me about his dreams of a simple life, close to the earth. We should get married and work the farm together, he said. I was flattered that he considered me the ideal companion for this undertaking and was tempted to join the dream for about a day. But when I told my mother about it, she promptly called Jonathan's mother and explained that her daughter had just turned seventeen and was nowhere near considering marriage.

For once, I approved of her gesture. The other mother, who had apparently been informed by her son, agreed with her, and that was the end of that. I don't know whether Jonathan ever went through with his plan for a dairy farm, as I lost track of him as soon as I left for New York.

Gerald, the other suitor, was a more serious prospect. He was in his midtwenties, and I think he knew my father before he knew me. He was already working, as an accountant or maybe a lawyer, I am no longer sure which, and invited me to dinners in good restaurants. He was an observant Jew (we never ordered chicken or meat, not kosher) and he showed great respect for my father, who approved of him without reservation. I believe Gerald was genuinely in love with me and was willing to wait for marriage until I finished college. He was a nice-looking young man, with sandy hair and a compact body. Unfortunately, I felt absolutely no physical attraction toward him. When he leaned over to kiss me as we sat in his car, all I saw were his prominent teeth. The idea of settling down with him in Chicago a few years hence struck me as absurd, but I was enough of a coquette, or sufficiently flattered by his attentions, not to tell him so. We corresponded for a while and spoke on the telephone a few times after I reached New York, but eventually I had to tell him the truth, or some version of it that I hoped would not hurt his feelings too much.

Why did I encourage these two young men before rejecting them? Freud speaks about female narcissism, which seeks only its own gratification and gives nothing in return: better to be loved than to love. I had had plenty of crushes on boys, always unrequited; to be the object of an unrequited love, for a change, must have appealed to me. Still, that sounds too calculating. It would be more accurate to say that I did not really trust, or even know, my own feelings. After all, why not think about starting a philosophical dairy farm in the Illinois countryside? Why not become the wife of a nice young lawyer (or accountant), whom my father approved of and who loved me? The possibility that I might truly fall in love with someone who also fell in love with me appeared like a far-off dream.

9

Fraternity Pin

Morningside Heights is like a small village, with its retail shops and restaurants stretching from 110th Street to 116th Street along Broadway. On the east side of Broadway, Columbia University takes over at 114th Street and stretches all the way to 125th. On the west side, Barnard College begins at 116th and ends at 120th. Most of the shops and restaurants have changed over the years, but the fruit and vegetable stands that spill out onto the sidewalk near the 110th Street subway entrance are still there, exactly as I have always remembered them. The Hungarian pastry shop on Amsterdam Avenue and 111th has had various owners over the years but is still in business, and the chocolate shop run by Viennese immigrants on Broadway and 114th Street still sells the same mouthwatering wares, although it must have changed hands by now. Each time I return to the neighborhood, to give a lecture or attend a conference at Columbia, I notice its small changes. Yet each time I feel as if I were returning home. Universities and their surroundings have been my home for more than sixty years now, and despite their differences they are also alike in many ways: crowds of young people carrying books or laptops, older people also carrying books or laptops, all of whom look familiar. Inside the academic buildings, corridors lined with faculty offices, bulletin boards loaded with posters announcing upcoming lectures, conferences, concerts, meetings. It adds up to a diverse yet homogeneous village that spans the globe. A curious realization, that despite my travels all over the world, I have lived most of my life in a village.

Of course, all this refers to before COVID. Will those lectures, concerts, and conferences be taking place in person in the coming years? Or will the convenience of Zoom, along with a genuine concern for the planet, make such events rare occurrences? Yet how sweet it is, to go to dinner with colleagues from other cities, other countries, curious about their world, after an afternooon of serious talk.

From the first day, I loved being at Barnard. My classes, the dorms, the "mixers" with Columbia boys, the get-togethers with other girls on my floor, when half a dozen of us would crowd into a small room to talk and find out more about each other—everything felt new and exciting, full of possibilities. I was Susan Rubin, a girl from Chicago. My childhood, my background, my immigrant family never entered the conversation—it was liberating. I had been assigned a single room on the top floor of Hewitt Hall, a long brick building running parallel to Broadway, with a large lawn in front. Hewitt was the longer part of an L whose short part was the other dorm, Brooks Hall. The two buildings were attached, with a single entrance in Brooks Hall. In 1956, all visitors had to sign in and wait downstairs—no admittance to the students' rooms except for visiting parents or siblings, and none at all for young men. After seven p.m., girls had to sign out and sign back in by eleven p.m. on weeknights, one a.m. on weekends. Long lines started to form on the front porch before the curfew on Saturday night, as girls said good night to their dates. We joked about returning to our prison but felt safe as we crossed the threshold and signed in.

That first semester, I enrolled in an introductory French literature course, just to maintain that connection—it was enjoyable but not revelatory, since the material was so close to home. My freshman English class, a requirement, was enlivened by a professor who did not hesitate to write caustic remarks next to sentences he considered sentimental or facile. One of the first papers I wrote, in which I gushed about discovering Culture with a capital *C* in New York City, came back with the notation *Culture, yes: like knowing how to pronounce Siobhan in Siobhan McKenna*. I had no idea who Siobhan McKenna was, and in the absence of the internet I had to rely on other sources to find out that she was a well-known Irish actress who was performing in New York that very month. Professor Bove had as his motto: *Out of every four adjectives, cut out three.* I liked him.

The first-year chemistry class was taught by a ramrod-straight white-haired woman, Helen Downing, who reminded me of my science teacher in junior high school: same no-nonsense attitude, eliciting the same devoted admiration from her students. In philosophy, I had chosen a course in logic, taught by a handsome gray-haired professor named Joseph Brennan, who taught us the name of every syllogism devised by medieval logicians. *Barbara*, for instance: All men are mortal, all Greeks are men, therefore all Greeks are mortal. (Oops, what about Greek women? In those days, that question made no sense.) Logic was like an extension of chemistry, a pursuit of categories where everything had its place, so deeply satisfying.

Above all, I loved my European history class, Europe from the Middle Ages to the Present. It was a yearlong course taught by a young professor named Louise Dalby, who had just gotten her doctorate at Harvard. I had not studied European history in high school, so her lectures were a revelation; in a way, it was my own history I was discovering. The Middle Ages, the Renaissance, the Reformation, the Industrial Revolution: knowledge consisted in putting names on things. Sándor Petőfi, the revolutionary poet whose verses I had recited in fourth grade in Budapest, was part of a Europe-wide movement, the revolution of 1848. Extraordinary! And in our own time, during those very days, a new revolution was taking place in Hungary. In late October, Hungarians descended into the streets, demanding reforms and greater independence from the Soviet Union. They failed, just as the revolutionaries of 1848 had failed and those of 1968 in Czechoslovakia would fail—until finally they succeeded, years later. Here was history in the making, and I was around to see it, even if only from afar.

Hungarian "freedom fighters," or just plain refugees who were called that, poured into New York City that fall, before heading to other places of welcome. I joined a campus committee to aid Hungarian students and met a young man named Attila, who became my friend before he headed to the University of Chicago. We lost touch after that, but for the first time, in talking with him in Hungarian, I felt a continuity between my former life, the life I had left behind with my red bicycle seven years earlier, and my life now. Was it possible that all the doors I had closed behind me would one day communicate with each other, creating an unbroken passage? This was not a question I asked myself at the time, and it was many years before the door to Hungary would truly reopen for me. But October 1956 provided an inkling that some connections can be remade, that not all departures are forever.

Meanwhile, dear reader, if you have accompanied me this far, you will not be surprised to learn that even though I had left New York only three years earlier, amid tearful goodbyes to the friends I was leaving behind, I made no effort that fall to reconnect with any of them. They were from a different time and Morningside Heights was another country, compared to East 81st Street. The only person I made a point of seeing was Granny, my darling granny who loved me so much. She had aged noticeably since we first arrived in New York, and soon she would no longer be able to live on her own; for a few months, however, until she left her apartment and the city to live with one or another of her children, I had a chance to visit her regularly. My visits were brief, but I rendered her the small service of cutting her toenails, which she could not reach. They were thick and misshapen, difficult to cut, but I derived a peculiar satisfaction from doing the job. (In 1956, there were no nail salons on practically every block in New York City.)

I met Aaron on a Saturday morning in September, while walking down Broadway with other Barnard and Columbia students on their way to Sabbath services. A small band had already formed, making its way down the hill to the Jewish Theological Seminary on 125th Street, and I found myself walking next to a boy with a round face I found attractive. He told me he was from Brookline, Massachusetts, where his father was the president of his congregation. Like me, he was a freshman, just getting settled in his dorm and his classes. He was pre-med, had always wanted to be a doctor, but was also enjoying his required courses in philosophy and literature, CC and Humanities. CC stood for contemporary civilization, which was something of a misnomer, because they started by reading Plato and Aristotle and did not arrive at Marx and Freud until second semester; in the humanities course, they began with Homer and ended with Dostoevsky. Barnard girls were not allowed to register for those famous courses, which defined what a well-educated college graduate (male) must have in his background, according to Columbia College. I told Aaron I wished I could take them as well, and recounted—with an ironic flourish—my high school fantasy of walking on a college campus talking about philosophy. He smiled: "You can talk about philosophy with me if you like."

By then we had arrived at JTS, and we sat next to each other during the service. I stole glances at him from time to time—he knew all the prayers and songs and sang them with enthusiasm. I felt a strange excitement that had very little to do with religion. Afterward, we walked back to 116th Street, and before we said goodbye he asked whether he could call me. I said yes and gave him the phone number on my floor. (Every floor had a phone in the hall, and whoever picked it up knocked on the door of the girl being called. There were few secrets in the dorm—we all knew who was receiving calls and when.)

A few days later, Aaron called and invited me to have coffee with him the following evening. It was a custom on weeknights to go to the Chock Full O'Nuts coffee shop on the corner of Broadway and 116th Street, in time to return by the eleven o'clock curfew. We sat at the counter and talked, oblivious to everyone around us. I told him a bit of my family's history, which seemed to interest him. As he accompanied me back to the entrance of Brooks Hall, he said he had been invited to a fraternity party on Saturday—would I like to go with him? I said I would, and practically danced my way to the elevator after saying goodbye.

At the party, I met some of Aaron's friends, including a lanky sophomore who struck me as very intelligent. But I had eyes only for Aaron. He seemed to be on good terms with everyone and was planning to join the fraternity. Everything about him thrilled me: the way he looked in his gray flannel slacks and navy blue blazer (he had always shopped at Brooks Brothers, he told me), his slight Boston accent (which I would recognize a few years later in the speeches of John F. Kennedy), his easygoing manner, his gentleness. I had known him only for a week but felt I could trust him.

After that, we saw each other several times a week. He would come over to the dorm after dinner and wait for me downstairs. Lining a hallway near the reception desk was a row of small rooms, hardly more than cubicles, each one outfitted with a small sofa and an armchair. They were known as "beau parlors," spaces where Barnard girls could receive their male guests. The rooms had no doors, and anyone passing by could look in and see what was happening—as I said, there were no secrets. Despite this glaring lack of privacy, the beau parlors were always in demand, for if you didn't find a free one you had to receive your guest in the large living room, even less private. Aaron and I were often lucky enough to find a parlor, and we would sit next to each other and talk. But after a few evenings we began to kiss, and I discovered, for the first time in my life, the power of sexual desire. All day long, even while raising my hand in class or making small talk with other girls in the cafeteria, I would be waiting for the moment when Aaron put his arm around me and leaned over to kiss me. I felt as if I were on fire and abandoned myself to the feeling with no thought about who might be watching. When a girl down the hall told me one day that she had seen me "petting pretty heavily" the night before, I just shrugged.

The truth is, I was astonishingly inexperienced in sexual matters, even for those repressed times. I had never "petted" before and had taken pride in being a girl with a sterling reputation. The idea of being thought "fast" appalled me. Yet here I was, smooching in the beau parlor with an ardor that ignored all obstacles. At the same time, it would never have occurred to me to "go all the way" (as we said then) with Aaron. Nice girls did not do that, in my view of the world. In reality, many Barnard girls did, already then, but I was unaware of it. I can be quite oblivious to what is happening around me, despite my father's advice about looking in all the mirrors while driving.

One weekend, I actually spent a night with Aaron, along with his sophomore fraternity brother and his date, in a house on Long Island that belonged to a friend of theirs. (I don't remember exactly how I got out of the curfew.) I suspected they had planned the overnight excursion with the idea that this would be Aaron's chance to get me into bed. But no matter how much I desired him, I did not want to have sex before marriage. That idea seems almost unbelievable now, except perhaps for strict Mormons or Evangelical Christians, but it was not totally preposterous back then. On some level, my prudishness may even have been a relief to Aaron, for he too was very young and probably inexperienced (we had never talked about sex). We slept in each other's arms that night, happy to be together.

I went home to Chicago over Christmas break and spent the whole vacation thinking about Aaron—I was sure he was doing the same about me. He had told me when we first met that I could talk to him about philosophy, but it had not taken me long to realize that philosophy was not his strong point. He was not an intellectual, did not get excited about ideas. I loved him for his uprightness and decency, quite aside from my deep physical attraction to him. He would make a very good doctor, I told myself. He did his course assignments assiduously; he cared deeply about his parents and his younger brother, who was slated to join him at Columbia in two years; he was a good friend to his fraternity brothers; and he was in love with me. Philosophy could wait. I could hardly believe my good fortune.

In January, final exams came and went. I saw Aaron almost every day, even if for just a few minutes between classes. On my way to meet him, I would sometimes ask myself how I could love him so much. To love was to want to give, with no thought of return. (Today, it's how I feel about my grandchildren.) I learned to knit and made him a long scarf of soft wool to protect him from the cold.

On a clear night in early February, I was suddenly awakened by singing. I opened my window and saw a group of young men standing on the lawn below. It was Aaron and his fraternity brothers, serenading me. The day before, he had asked me to become "pinned" to him—that is, to accept his fraternity pin as a sign of our commitment to each other. I had said yes, with stars in my eyes—but to be serenaded was beyond my wildest dreams! I could not run downstairs, since the doors were locked, but I threw kisses. Many girls stuck their heads out their windows and clapped. It was even better than an engagement.

The next day, I started wearing the fraternity pin on my sweater. Girls came up and congratulated me; I felt like the heroine of a true romance. In the evening, I called my parents and did my best to explain to them what being pinned meant. They did not understand the fine points, but they could tell how happy I was. I had already told them about Aaron, who seemed to them like a very desirable young man. We made a tentative plan that they and my sister would drive with me to New York after spring break and I would introduce Aaron to the whole family. When I told him about it, he appeared happy. I assumed he had told his parents about me and that they were equally pleased.

I flew home over spring break and was received with great excitement, with *ohh*s and *ahh*s about the pretty black-and-gold pin. Daddy was thrilled that Aaron came from an observant Jewish home, and Mother was thrilled that he would be a doctor. Maybe for the first time since we had arrived in the United States, I felt a simple, uncomplicated happiness and harmony. My parents approved of me, my little sister looked up to me, and my future stretched ahead like a well laid-out map. I would marry Aaron after we both graduated from college, or maybe even before then (not unheard of, in those days), and work as a chemist while he attended medical school. After he finished, we would have children who would be part of a close-knit American family from Boston, and when the kids started school I would resume my career.

I shared the driving with Daddy on our trip east, and we arrived in New York late in the evening. My parents and sister were staying in a hotel and I went back to my dorm, eager to speak with Aaron. We had a date to meet the following afternoon, with my family.

On the phone, he sounded slightly awkward. "Look, I think we'd better meet first tomorrow, just you and I. Okay?" Okay, I said. Was there something wrong, I wondered. But I reassured myself: Aaron loved me, there was no reason to worry. We met on a bench on the lawn in front of Hewitt Hall the next morning; Aaron's round face, usually so open and smiling, looked clouded. "Susan, you know I love you," he began, as if it were a rehearsed speech. "But while I was home, my parents reminded me that we are so very young—you're not even eighteen, and I just turned nineteen. We're practically children! They strongly urged me to slow down." Seeing my stricken face, he hurried on: "This doesn't mean we'll stop seeing each other, not at all. I just think my parents are right and we shouldn't start planning our wedding! It's probably best for me not to meet your parents just yet. I'm really sorry, I know they drove all the way from Chicago so we could meet. I hope you understand." He fell silent, looking uneasy.

What I understood was that the dream was over. Aaron had returned home for spring break and, being the good and loving son he was, had listened to the advice of his parents. Of course, they were right. Hadn't my own mother said similar words just a few months earlier to the mother of my unlikely suitor Jonathan?

Yes, but that was different. This felt like an abandonment. He said he loved me, but I no longer believed him. I slowly undid the pin on my blouse and handed it to him. "Yes, I understand. It's best if I return this to you." He took it and put in his pocket. I stood up. "Maybe we can have coffee tomorrow night," he said. "Yes, maybe," I replied, and walked away.

I had not cried while he was there and did not cry afterward either, but I felt crushed and humiliated. *If I don't get used to this, I'll die!* What would I tell my parents? I tried to make light of it, but Mother saw immediately how deeply hurt I was. Unfortunately, her way of trying to make me feel better consisted of the following: "Probably his parents made inquiries and decided we weren't good enough. You told him Daddy is a rabbi, but they must have heard he was a *shammes*." Great! We didn't measure up, and it was all my fault. I gritted my teeth and kept silent. I just wanted them to leave me alone and return to Chicago. They drove back the next day, without even having seen Morningside Heights.

I did not meet Aaron for coffee the following evening, and saw him only a few more times that spring. We tried to act as if nothing had changed, save for the detail of the pin. But for me, everything had changed. I no longer trusted him and began to view him critically: he didn't like to talk about what he was reading in Humanities or CC, and his fraternity parties bored me. Gradually, we stopped seeing each other. By the end of spring semester I was no longer attending Sabbath services, preferring to spend my Saturday mornings at the library; by the end of sophomore year, I no longer kept kosher (until then, I had eaten only fish in the cafeteria), and on Saturday afternoons I would often take the subway to the Metropolitan Opera and buy a standing-room ticket. Aaron's and my paths did not cross again.

Then, one day in the fall of senior year, not long after my father died, I suddenly received a phone call from Aaron. He wanted to know how I was, what had happened to me over the past two years. We met for coffee at Chock Full O'Nuts, he still wearing Brooks Brothers flannels and blazer. I don't remember what I wore. He told me he was taking his medical boards soon and applying to medical school, as he had always planned. "I'm not much of a reader, I'm afraid," he said with a little laugh. After the required courses of freshman year, he had stuck close to the pre-med curriculum, with no time for philosophy or literature.

I was impressed by his frankness, his sense of his own limitations—and could only wonder at the love I had once felt for him. I told him about my father, and he expressed genuine sympathy. He was still the upright young man I had known; it was I who had changed. Or had I? Maybe I would always be the five-year-old child determined to survive, to outlive any abandonment—always abandoning first, so as not to be abandoned. When he walked me back to the dorm, I knew I would never see him again, and I never did. But I searched for him on the internet recently, as I was writing these pages, and found that he had retired after a long career as a surgeon in a suburb of Chicago. There was mention of his beloved wife of many years, and of a daughter.

I sometimes wonder what my life would have been like if I had not felt so wounded, if we had continued to see each other and gotten married by senior year, as some of my classmates had done. Would we have had a happy marriage, with children, as I had dreamed? The fraternity pin had been a badge of belonging, just as Aaron himself represented the normalcy I had always yearned for in America. Once I had returned the pin and found him wanting, there was no way back.

After the fiasco with Aaron, the end of spring semester arrived quickly, with final exams and papers to write. For my English class I wrote my first research paper, on the meteoric rise and the just-as-sudden fall of an eighteenth-century politician named John Wilkes, who interested me because of all his contradictions: he was a radical who turned conservative, an ugly man known to be a rake, a hero of the people who quashed a popular uprising. Writing that paper kept me up all night for several nights and started me on smoking, but I felt enormous satisfaction when it was done. I was planning to be a chemistry major (heaven knows why, since the courses I really loved were all in the humanities), but the pleasure of doing research and then shaping it into a piece of writing gave me a sense of what a creative life might be. (I know, chemistry can be creative too, but not for beginners.) The process of writing is often painful, hampered by self-doubt, but oh, the satisfaction when you succeed in finding the right words! That feeling should have taught me something about myself, about what I really wanted in life. Instead, I barreled ahead, unreflectively, on the path I had set.

By the time I returned home for the summer, I had almost convinced myself that Aaron was just a memory. My mother still spoke about him occasionally, but I discouraged her. I had not forgiven her for her remark about our not being good enough for his parents, and once again felt toward her as I had in high school: she and I had nothing in common. In reality, her remark had touched a nerve. Maybe the question was not whether we were good enough for Aaron's family, but whether I was American enough to want to live the life he promised with his fraternity pin. Maybe my dream of happy integration into his Jewish American clan had always been only a pipe dream.

Best not to go there; it was no time to dwell on the past. I had to find a job for the summer, as we had agreed when my parents accepted to send me to Barnard. Meanwhile, we sat down every night to our dinner of broiled chicken and mixed vegetables (frozen), which Mother had decided was the right diet for Daddy's heart condition: low in fat as well as easy to make. Gone were the days when she would cook chicken paprikas and *nockerli*, those plump noodles that tasted so good in the fatty sauce, or bake the delicious pastries filled with poppy seed paste. She was right to watch his diet, but how dull those dinners were!

After a week of searching, I found a job as a typist in a large insurance company downtown. I did not tell them I would be leaving at the end of the summer, did not even mention I had attended college—that was the advice of the employment agency I had consulted. "They'll never hire you if they know it's temporary," the woman told me. So I lied, told them I had spent the past year with relatives in New York. The job did not require much training other than typing skills, which I had acquired in high school. It consisted of sending out form letters to clients who were behind on their premium payments, mechanical and boring. The office was one huge room lined with rows of desks, and even the manager, who had a title like *vice president*, had only a cubicle in one corner, not a separate room; it was not a fancy firm. On my first day on the job, the manager welcomed me and told me I was the first Jewish girl he had hired. He said it quite proudly, as if I should commend him for it.

Despite the deadly boredom, I liked the job because it was in the Loop and during my lunch hour I could walk to the public library, whose main branch in the style of an Italian palazzo occupied a whole block on Michigan Avenue, or to the Art Institute a few blocks down. My English professor had mocked me for gushing about Culture, but for me the feeling was real. I found enormous comfort in entering those grand buildings knowing that I belonged there, that it was where my real life took place. Those quiet rooms full of people reading or looking at works of art represented something admirable, something to strive for. They were the antidote to the dullness and frustration of the office and of life at home.

My other source of comfort that summer, as had been the case so often before, was reading. We had discussed one of Thomas Mann's stories in my freshman English class, *Tonio Kröger*, about the dark-haired young man who feels like a stranger wherever he goes. It had left a deep impression on me, maybe because Mann's protagonist was a divided soul who became a writer. Writers succeed in turning self-division into words. I was only a reader, but I could identify with that. Soon I had devoured *Buddenbrooks*, Mann's first novel, based on his own family story, which dwells on the clash between the upstanding but dull *bürgers* who create the wealth of a German merchant family and their more artistically inclined descendants. The last of the Buddenbrooks dies while still a teenager, but he shares with Tonio Kröger a dreaminess of character and an artistic bent that put him at odds with his powerful father and with the family tradition. Mann was clearly fascinated by such contradictions.

That summer, I embarked on *The Magic Mountain*, which I had been told was Mann's masterpiece. Once again, it was a story of contradictions, this time expanded to huge philosophical proportions. The novel's hero, Hans Castorp, is a likable but very ordinary young man (as the narrator keeps reminding us), who becomes transformed—or one might say refined, the way raw metal is refined into gold—over the course of the seven years he spends in a sanatorium in the Swiss Alps. One thing that keeps him there is his infatuation with another patient, a woman from the eastern reaches of the Russian Empire, whose "Kirghiz eyes" remind him of a boy he had worshipped from afar when he was in school. This bit of gender ambiguity completely escaped me at the time, as did Mann's stereotyped portrayal of Hans's love object, Clavdia, who is described as "Asiatic" in contrast to Hans's solid Germanness. Her effect on him is like

that of a spell in a fairy tale, or of a femme fatale. The magic
comes crashing down, however, when World War I breaks out
and propels Hans Castorp back to the reality of the everyday
world, just as that world is about to be destroyed—along with
Hans himself, and all the other young men who are fed to the
fire. By the time Mann wrote the novel, just a few years after the
war, the world he portrays appeared like an epoch in the distant
past, he observes in his preface.

One reason I loved Mann is that he made me feel intelligent. *The Magic Mountain* is rife with speculations about time
and death and illness, and their relation to genius. Aside from
Hans's love for the captivating Clavdia, what keeps him on the
mountaintop during all those years is his fascination with two
other patients, Settembrini and Naphta, who spend their days
arguing about philosophy. Settembrini is Italian, a humanist, a
great believer in progress, rationality, and the Enlightenment;
Naphta is a Polish Jew educated by Jesuits, who sees the world
as a struggle between Good and Evil, with humans bending
toward the irrational. Mann does not say which of them is
right, although most commentators think he favors the humanist Settembrini, but clearly he is also drawn to the nihilist
Naphta, whose tormented soul is akin to artistic genius. The
artist is never very far, in Mann's estimation, from illness and
from the demonic. Yet another contradiction, since outwardly
Mann himself led a very proper bourgeois life. (His diaries reveal
a more tormented personality, especially on account of his sexual
attraction to young men.)

A few years ago, I discovered that Susan Sontag had idolized Mann as a precocious high school student in Los Angeles.
To her mind he represented European culture, at a time when
Southern California was not exactly a highbrow paradise. I was
reading him just ten years later, in a Chicago that felt like a desert
too. Mann's writing was a lifeline, a promise that there was more

to life than typing form letters in a cavernous office all day and eating broiled chicken at night, with a family I felt estranged from. One can be insufferably arrogant when one is eighteen.

Still, if Mann had become the alibi for my arrogance, I now realize that he may have represented to me not so much European culture (unlike Sontag, I did not attach a geographical qualification to culture, even if all of my cultural references were European) as Europe itself, the land where I had been a child and where I had known my first home. I had spent a number of years and no small effort forgetting that place, leaving it behind; Mann's magic mountaintop offered me a first step back to it.

10

Beethoven Concerto

At the end of the summer, I announced at the insurance company that I had decided to move to New York. People wished me well, and I left for Barnard with a feeling of relief and anticipation.

The next two years were spent in doggedly pursuing my major in chemistry, ticking off all the required courses, including physics and advanced math. I cannot understand exactly why I put myself through that, unless it was to prove that I could do it (in my physics class, which I had to take at Columbia, I was the only girl), or out of sheer stubbornness. I still liked chemistry well enough and derived satisfaction from its orderliness, but there was an element of self-punishment in my pursuit that puzzles me. Self-punishment for what crime? Or was I testing myself, to see how well I could survive? But this sounds too melodramatic. I was probably just trodding my way, with blinkers on, until finally one day I said "Enough."

I recently obtained my transcript from Barnard to see the details. In sophomore year, it was Qualitative Analysis in chemistry and Trigonometry in math, followed by Quantitave Analysis and Calculus I; the next year, Organic Chemistry, Calculus II,

Physics, Calculus III—but in the spring of junior year, I dropped that math course. It was integral calculus, where I could no longer visualize the functions and the curves. Until then, in the calculus courses, I could always imagine a function as a little Fn character that moved, and the curve as the map of its movement. Now, everything had become more abstract and I could no longer follow Fn's story.

In other words, it all came down to literature: story. Years later, when I became enamored of the new literary theories based on structural analysis, I realized that my science and math background had not been a total waste. Categories and typologies, the stuff of structuralism, were familiar territory. But still, all those hours and days and months spent on physics and chemistry, when I could have been reading Milton! (I never did read *Paradise Lost*, one of the many gaps in my literary education.)

The dropping of the calculus course was dated March 3, 1959, on the transcript, halfway through the spring semester of junior year. But my change of direction had actually begun a year earlier, when I enrolled in a course on the Faust myth in European literature. It was taught by Elizabeth Wilkinson, from University College London, who had been named the first Gildersleeve Visiting Professor at Barnard. Virginia Gildersleeve had been a long-serving dean at the college and a pioneering woman in academia; the professorship in her honor invited a distinguished woman scholar to Barnard for a semester. Elizabeth Wilkinson was around fifty at the time, and she arrived from England with an aura of glamor, preceded by an article about her in the *New York Times*. I had studied with a number of women faculty at Barnard, but she appeared to me to be on a different level. She delivered polished, erudite lectures, even while projecting an air of kindness and friendliness—this, I realized, was what true authority looked like. She was an academic star, a very rare status for a woman at that time. She became my role model, although we did not use that terminology then.

The material she taught was special as well. The story of Faust's bargain with the Devil goes very far back in the European imagination: the striving for ever-new experiences, the willingness to take dangerous risks, the desire for eternal youth, all those ideas were with us still, Professor Wilkinson explained. No wonder that some of Europe's greatest writers had written their version of the Faust legend: Marlowe, Goethe, Thomas Mann, we read them all. But despite her many virtues, Elizabeth Wilkinson was a woman of her time: not even the shadow of a gender question entered into her expert analyses of those works. Could women ever strive for knowledge and achievement the way Faust did? Or were they destined to be only Margarete, the innocent and beautiful object (and victim) of male desire? Such questions, which would preoccupy me and other feminist theorists twenty years later, were never raised, and I am sorry to report that they never occurred to me either. I was too busy acquiring the canon to start questioning it just yet.

Not surprisingly, I chose to write my final paper on Mann's *Dr. Faustus*. If *The Magic Mountain* had enthralled me, this book awed me. Mann's Faust figure is a composer, a musical genius, and as part of his story Mann presents pages and pages of technical analyses of works by Beethoven and other musical giants, as well as of the fictional works he imagines his hero to be composing. How had Mann learned all that? My admiration knew no bounds. But the really awe-inspiring aspect of that novel, for me, was its historical and political subtext. Mann, Professor Wilkinson explained, had been an outspoken and courageous anti-Nazi who had left Germany when Hitler came to power. (He had died just a few years earlier, in 1955.) *Dr. Faustus* could be read as his anguished attempt to understand what had allowed Germany—and in particular, German intellectuals—to sell their soul to the devil of Nazism. As usual, Mann provides no easy answers, but that makes his work all the more powerful. I wrote my paper in a fever of excitement and creativity, and it was then that I realized how much more compelling this activity—reading great literature and writing about it—felt to me than doing experiments in a chemistry lab.

Still, I soldiered on with the chemistry major for another whole year, until that break with the math course showed me what I had to do. By then it was too late to switch my major, since I had already satisfied all the requirements in chemistry. But my mind was made up: I would attend summer school to study literature, and devote my senior year to literature as well, in French and English. I would definitely not aim for a career as a chemist. Maybe as a science writer? I turned that thought around in my head for several weeks, thinking to salvage at least a small part of all that scientific education. But the passion I felt was for novels and poetry, which occupied your emotions as well as your intelligence. Science did not do that, at least not for me.

After I informed my parents of my decision over the telephone, my father flew to New York to talk with me. "Your mother and I are worried about you," he said—a rare show of unanimity in their views. Since I was convinced at the time that Mother would never understand me, this was not a propitious beginning for our conversation. I still felt close to Daddy, however, and it touched me that he had made the trip just to see me. I asked him why he was worried. "This sudden change from chemistry to literature, where will it get you? What can you do after graduation? You don't have the luxury of not working, and besides, I know you want a career. Maybe if you were married . . ." His voice trailed off, and then he resumed and said brightly: "Maybe you could go to law school."

"But I don't want to be a lawyer," I replied. "Right now, I just want to study literature."

"You don't come from a wealthy family," he said. "What can you do with literature?" I confessed that I had no idea—but there was still another whole year of college, plenty of time to wait and see. And as far as marriage was concerned, he shouldn't worry—there wasn't anyone I wanted to marry at the moment, but I had plenty of dates.

It was true, I did have plenty of dates. I had even had a serious romance with another Columbia pre-med student that year, who unlike Aaron was truly interested in philosophy and was a fan of Thomas Mann. He was part of a group of Jewish boys from Brooklyn, many of them the sons of immigrants and the first in their family to attend college, who commuted to Morningside Heights by subway every day. They were intense and brilliant, and my boyfriend Alex was the most intense of all. I loved listening to his extended riffs about music and literature, which were almost like classroom lectures. Like several other members of his circle, Alex was preparing to be a doctor, but he had clearly benefited from the required humanities courses at the college and had followed them up with more advanced seminars. He was a genuine intellectual, passionate about ideas and eager to argue about them.

Unfortunately, I did not feel much sexual attraction toward this brilliant young man, and after a halfhearted attempt to become a couple, we decided to simply remain friends. But I did not tell my father this. Nor did I tell him that I too worried about what I would do after graduation. I was very much aware that I had no one to rely on financially after college, but I wanted to spend my last year feeling happy, finally studying what gave me the greatest pleasure. After some more wheedling on my part, Daddy agreed that after returning home I would attend summer school at the University of Wisconsin in Madison, where I had found course offerings on Shakespeare and Joyce. That would still leave me time to work for a month before senior

year started. He returned to Chicago, not totally reassured about my prospects but willing to support me in my plan. And if he said yes, Mother would follow.

While I had been struggling with the direction of my life, Granny had exited hers. She died at our home in Chicago in April 1959 and was buried the next day as required by Jewish law. I did not even have a chance to attend her funeral. She had been ill for some time, living with my aunt Magdi's family before she moved to us. I had seen her over spring break and noticed her shrunken appearance—it was cancer, Mother told me. What I think is the last photo of her shows her reclining in a rocking chair on what looks like the porch of a summer house. She is smiling, her face still smooth and her brow unwrinkled, an old woman at peace with herself. She must have known she was dying, however. On the back of the photo, the inscription in Hungarian reads: *To my dear good children with true love, their sick mother.* It is undated but appears to be from the summer of 1958, when she was eighty years old. She had just turned eighty-one when she died.

Proust's narrator recounts his beloved grandmother's death and tells us that he felt no real sadness at the time, but years later, returning to the hotel in the seaside resort where he had spent several summers with her as an adolescent, he is suddenly caught in an ocean of grief as he bends down to fasten his shoe. Flooded with the memory of how much she had loved him, he finally mourns his grandmother. Our emotional response to a deep loss can come upon us unexpectedly only much later, he muses. Proust calls this disconnect between the event and its emotional impact the intermittences of the heart.

I wish I could say that I too had such an intermittence, mourning my grandmother years after her death. But that would be a lie. When I learned the news on that April day, from a phone call I took in the hallway outside my room in Brooks Hall, I did not cry. She had stopped being a large presence in my life years ago, yet I mourned her in my own way. The girl down the hall owned a record player and some records. I told her about my grandmother and asked if I could listen to Heifetz playing the Beethoven violin concerto. Sympathetic, she said, "Of course," then left me alone.

Outside, the sun was setting over the Hudson, burnt orange and purple. I put on the record. At first it was only the orchestra playing, and I waited for the violin to enter—then it did, and from there on it was a dialogue, now the violin responding to the orchestra's melody, now the orchestra amplifying the violin's. The long first movement ended with a bang and the adagio began like a dirge—but suddenly, with no warning whatsoever, the violin began a lilting melody, like a smile after tears. I thought about my grandmother. She had lived through two world wars, buried her husband at age forty-five, lost her first-born son to the Nazis, crossed the Atlantic when she was almost seventy. During her last years in New York, before she became too sick to live alone, she had had a suitor. They sat together on a park bench near the East River every afternoon. She had laughed when she told me this: "Just think, at my age," but I could tell that she was very pleased. She had wispy light brown hair, even at the end, and very proud of it too, vain old woman. *Don't die, I love you!*

When the music stopped, I turned off the record player and went back to my room. Dry-eyed, I wondered whether the calm I felt was the result of an emotional flaw (we had read a book in French class about a man who didn't cry at his mother's funeral), or whether it was caused by the music—as if all the sorrow had been channeled, absorbed into the violin.

As it turned out, my mourning for my grandmother was a dress rehearsal for a much greater loss. My father was only forty-nine years old.

11

Wooden Bench, Lake Michigan

I do not often dwell on death or on my own mortality, even now that the years still remaining to me are rapidly shrinking. This may account for my persistent (some would say mindless) optimism, my unflagging ability to put the past behind me and walk on, a trait widespread among immigrants and people with painful childhoods who "make good despite it all." Psychologists call it resilience, but I sometimes think of it as callousness, an inability—or unwillingness—to *feel* pain. It is as if the feeling, if fully allowed in and recognized, might end up engulfing you, make you drown in sorrow. Can one really die of sorrow? I have never wanted to find out.

For a long time, I put my father's death behind me, after the first shock. But he came back to me in dreams. My mother, who died when she was about to turn eighty, always appears young and healthy in my dreams. My father appears propped up on a pillow in his hospital bed, dying. He died in the middle of the night, with no loved one near him.

I am now more than three decades older than he was when he departed from this world. Of him it can truly be said that he had an untimely death. In one sense, all deaths are untimely, for who leaves this world having accomplished everything they had hoped for? What haunts me is that he died alone, and that by all indications he was ready to die. *Ten years earlier, when the doctors gave him up, he made my mother put a copy of the Talmud under his pillow and told her fiercely not to cry. This time, he packed a small suitcase and put his papers in order,* I once wrote. But if that is so, then was his death untimely? Maybe he felt he had accomplished all he could. A few weeks earlier, we had taken a walk together after I had returned home for the summer, and he had confided to me that he felt at loose ends, not sure what his next steps should be. Maybe he was done.

Recently, in a small suitcase full of my mother's photos and papers at my sister's house, I found two tattered pages from a newspaper, front pages of the weekly *National Jewish Post*, Chicago edition. The first one, dated August 28, 1958, features a large photo at the top of the page, above a headline: *$20,000 From a Shul to a School.* The article states that Congregation Anshe Pinsk has made that gift to the Central Hebrew Day School. The photo shows my father dressed in a dark suit, smiling, flanked by two men on either side; a man on his right is handing a check to a man on his left, and there is an insert of the check itself, with the amount clearly showing. Twenty thousand dollars was a large sum in those days, and the Central Hebrew Day School would use it to jump-start its campaign to build another wing. My father, who was the executive director of the school, had been instrumental in obtaining the money and he was justly proud of his work. The caption beneath the photo identifies him as the man in the center of the group; the man on his left, receiving the check, is the school's president. The second tattered page is dated exactly one year later: August 28, 1959. In the middle of the page, beneath the featured story about the Israeli prime minister Golda Meir's upcoming trip to the United States, is a short article titled "School Grieves Rabbi

M. Rubin." The article begins: *Students at the Central Hebrew day school as well as the entire Jewish community are mourning the death of Rabbi Michael N. Rubin, Aug. 17, while on a visit to his sisters in Toronto, Canada.* The writer gets a few facts wrong, but the gist is there: before becoming executive director, Rabbi Rubin had taught advanced Hebrew classes at the school for several years, and in Budapest he had been secretary of the Orthodox Jewish Community Bureau. He had resided at 909 W. Winona Street and was survived by his wife and two daughters, as well as his sisters.

What the obituary did not state was the essential: he was a good man full of contradictions, like most of us.

I will not write the detailed story of his death again, having already written it once long ago. But I am not ready to let it go. Georges Perec, a French writer I admire, wrote an autobiographical book in which he reproduced a few of his earlier texts, with footnotes and commentaries from his later perspective. Footnotes and commentaries are my bread and butter, as the saying goes; I will therefore follow Perec's example and reproduce my earlier account here, from *Budapest Diary*, with today's accompaniments. (Instead of actual footnotes, my notations appear between parentheses.)

My father had monthly appointments with a heart specialist downtown, who charged him less than his other patients because he was an immigrant and a man of learning. On his visit in late July, the doctor told him his electrocardiogram did not look good; he should go into the hospital. But my father worried about life insurance. He had just taken out another policy for five thousand dollars, and he hadn't told them about his heart condition. He decided to go to the hospital in Toronto, where his sister, my aunt Rózsi, lived.

Did he figure he could die in Canada without our losing the five thousand dollars? Ten years earlier, when the doctors gave him up, he made my mother put a copy of the Talmud under his pillow and told her fiercely not to cry. This time, he packed a small suitcase and put his papers in order.

I drove him to the airport—it was still Midway then. I asked why he didn't go to the hospital in Chicago. "It's better this way," he said. When he reached the plane, crossing a strip of airfield and climbing the steps, he turned around and waved to me. He wore a wide-brimmed summer hat so that I couldn't see his eyes, but his mouth was smiling. Then he went inside the plane and did not look back. (I never saw him alive again—and still cannot understand what twisted logic made him fly to Toronto. If a doctor who knows you and that you trust tells you you must go into the hospital, do you respond by leaving the country? In Toronto, no doctor knew him. Maybe, expecting to die, he wanted to make sure Mother had some money to live on—but if so, why did she go along with that idea? Or did he hope to survive and return to Chicago recuperated, still holding his life insurance policy?)

A few days later he called from Toronto. His voice on the telephone sounded exhausted, each word a huge effort. I tried to imagine him in his hospital bed, his head on the pillow with the receiver cradled against his shoulder. For years afterward he appeared to me that way in dreams, always sounding as if he were dying.

He asked me to come to see him but said first I should drive to the cottage and spend the weekend with my mother and sister. (Actually, that last phone call came almost two weeks after he left. As far as I have been able to reconstruct it, he arrived in Toronto on Friday, July 31; spent the long weekend at Aunt Rózsi's house [Monday, August 3, was a national holiday in Canada]; and entered Mount Sinai Hospital on Tuesday, August 4, or Wednesday, August 5. He called me on Thursday, August 13, the day before my summer school session ended. His prolonged hospital stay appeared useless; in 1959, coronary bypass surgery had not yet been invented, but I still wonder whether he could have received better care.)

"I'd like to fly to Toronto right away," I said.

"Your mother wants to see you. A few days won't matter," he replied. So I packed up the car and drove to the small town on Lake Michigan. (As in other years, my father had gotten a job leading the Sabbath services in a resort, in exchange for a summer house.)

I reached the cottage on Friday afternoon. After the first warm greetings, my mother began the usual reproaches: I was too fat, read too much, didn't care about her. I maintained an ironic silence. Then she told me she had to go to Chicago on Monday and was counting on me to stay with my sister. That loosened my tongue, for I had planned to fly to Toronto on Monday. A scene ensued, with both of us mouthing our well-rehearsed lines.

I: "You're petty, mean-spirited, will never understand me." She: "You're a monster of selfishness. If your father's in the hospital, it's because of you. He worries about you all the time, even on his sickbed."

I finally agreed to wait an extra day.

Monday morning, I drove her to the train station. The rest of the day I swam and picked wild blackberries with my sister. That night, after my mother came home, we succeeded in avoiding a fight and went to bed early. I was packed to leave the next morning.

In my sleep, I heard the telephone ring. It was my aunt from Toronto. "You should all come," she said. Her voice sounded calm, but the words came slowly, as if choked. She did not say at first that he was dead, only kept repeating we should all come.

"If we come right away, will we see him alive?" I asked.

She waited. Finally she said in a low voice: "No."

He had died earlier that night, alone in his room. They had called her from the hospital when they noticed it.

"We had no idea how seriously ill he was! He didn't tell anyone, not even the doctors." She sounded at once reproachful and pleading, as if asking to be forgiven for not being there when he died. The funeral would be the next day, in accordance with Orthodox law.

I drove us all to Midway Airport. We stopped at a gas station to go to the bathroom, and my sister asked me if we would ever see our father again. We would not see him, but we could think about him, I told her. She started to cry, and I felt angry at myself.

I felt especially angry at my mother. She had stopped me from seeing him; now it was too late. She sobbed all the way to the airport, while I watched her in hate and silence. I wanted to hit her. (It occurs to me that Mother's errand in Chicago may have been more urgent than selfish—so urgent that Daddy himself felt it necessary to call me from his hospital bed, instructing me to put off my trip to Toronto. I will never know what that errand was, just as I will never know why he did not tell his sister how sick he was, or why he had decided not to try and save his life.)

Our plane landed in Toronto at noon. When my mother saw my aunt, she burst into loud wails. What would become of her and her daughters, especially the little one? I said nothing while my aunt spoke to her soothingly. She drove us to her house. My uncle was there, with some Hungarian friends who had known my father. My aunt and I got back in the car to go see about the funeral arrangements.

We drove to the place where my father's body was. He was laid out in a bare wooden coffin as prescribed by the Law, wrapped in a white robe of fine cotton with lace trim around the collar, the robe he wore to synagogue on the High Holidays. (Did we stop to pick it up in Chicago on the way to the airport? Or had he packed it in his suitcase?) His face looked beautiful, like that of a very young man. He was forty-nine years old. The skin was soft and smooth and bore no makeup. I looked at him until my aunt pulled me away, and for the first time I cried.

The funeral took place that afternoon. It was hot and sunny. We watched them lower the coffin into the ground. The rabbi chanted the required prayer. My mother cried hysterically. I wore a borrowed black dress that felt too tight across my breasts. (My sister, who was eight and a half years old, was not allowed to attend the funeral, and she reproached us for it often in later years. In 1988, after our mother died, she had my father's coffin transferred, with my consent, to the cemetery in Connecticut where Mother was buried.)

Reading this account as if it were a literary text written by someone else, I am struck by how much negative emotion is directed at the mother. It is almost as if the daughter's conflict with her mother overshadowed her grief at her father's death. She cries only once, when she sees her father's body laid out for the burial—and she is not with her mother then, but with her beloved aunt. It is as if she choked up all her feelings in her effort not to resemble her "hysterical" mother. But it would be wrong to blame the mother for the daughter's inability to grieve properly. As we know, this daughter has a tendency to bottle up her feelings, to grit her teeth and move on. The "If I don't get used to this, I'll die" syndrome that she first experienced when she was five years old has served her on other occasions of loss and sorrow over the years. It has proved to be an efficient defense against drowning, as she sometimes puts it to herself, but it also has its drawbacks, as she herself is aware. The numbing of feelings, the resistance to true intimacy with another are among the results of such bottling-up. Someone who loved her once said to her, long ago: "You've built such high walls around yourself that nobody can scale them." And then he left—but that's another story.

After the funeral in Toronto and the prescribed week of mourning (sitting shiva in my aunt's house in the borrowed black dress; many people coming by to offer condolences, to which I cannot respond properly), my mother and I flew back to Chicago, leaving my sister in Aunt Rózsi's care for a few weeks. It had been decided, over late-night discussions around the kitchen table, that Mother and Judy would move to New York, since there was no one left for them in Chicago. In New York they would be near Mother's sister, my aunt Magdi, who had recently immigrated with her husband from Montreal. Uncle Laci and his wife were in New York too, when they were not traveling, and I would be in my last year at Barnard. From then on, my mother never lived more than a few miles from her sister and, after all the siblings had moved to Miami, from her brothers as well. The family sustained her, as it had often done before.

Our task in Chicago was to empty the apartment, give away Daddy's library of Hebrew books (we entrusted them to the relative who had gotten Daddy his first job in Chicago six years earlier), and then pack up the car with what was left: clothes, a bit of silverware, a few books, and miscellaneous papers and photographs. There was no time to spend on grieving, or so I must have told myself. But I clearly remember sitting alone on a wooden bench on the shore of Lake Michigan on the afternoon of September 1, watching the whitecaps on the steel-gray water and thinking about the start of the Second World War. Exactly twenty years earlier, when I was six weeks old, Hitler had invaded Poland and set in motion the events that would land me on that bench and my father in his grave. History, with its capital *H* and big axe. Cutting.

As I have often done since then in moments of great pain, I deflected the feeling into abstract reflection. *After great pain, a formal feeling comes.* Emily Dickinson wrote that, but I had not read Emily Dickinson yet. Instead, I murmured the opening lines of W. H. Auden's "September 1, 1939":

> I sit in one of the dives
> On Fifty-second Street
> Uncertain and afraid
> As the clever hopes expire
> Of a low dishonest decade.

These lines seem oddly pertinent today, almost a century later. But while Auden, like Beethoven in his violin concerto, plumbs the depths of negation and despair, he too manages to end his poem on a hopeful note:

> Defenseless under the night

Our world in stupor lies;
Yet, dotted everywhere,
Ironic points of light
Flash out wherever the Just
Exchange their messages:
May I, composed like them
Of Eros and of dust,
Beleaguered by the same
Negation and despair,
Show an affirming flame.

Why are the points of light ironic? Because hope must always come with a tinge of irony, the awareness of its own fragility. Hope for the best and expect the worst, the ironist's motto.

Then I thought of Auden's homage to W. B. Yeats, who had died earlier that same year, 1939:

Earth, receive an honoured guest.
William Yeats is laid to rest.

My father had not been a great poet, but he too had striven and was now at rest.

On our two-day drive to New York, I began to think of my mother as no longer my enemy. True, she would never understand me, but once I came fully to terms with that thought (a process that took several years), our fundamental differences in temperament—or what I took to be that—no longer infuriated me. In a sense, our difference made me feel more kindly toward her, the way one feels toward an old friend one has grown apart from but still treats with affection. She was my mother, after all. Over the years that followed, I did not confide in her or seek her advice but tried not to rage at her either—something I only half succeeded in, I confess. I knew she loved me and wanted to see me happy. If I could not love her back as fully as she deserved, at least I could be kind.

On the second day of our trip, sitting next to me in the passenger seat, Mother told me the story of her first love, who (as I should have suspected) had not been Daddy. The young man was her age, tall and good-looking, and his parents owned a grocery store not far from her house. "He was sweet and tender, and loved me dearly," she remembered with a lilt in her voice (she was speaking Hungarian). "Unfortunately, his parents had no money and neither did we, so they wanted a rich wife for him. When he broke it all off, I wanted to die—I became so depressed I ended up in the hospital. It was only when Magdi told me she was expecting a baby, your cousin Agnes, that I finally got out of my depression." Agnes was born in February 1935; Mother's love affair must have come to its painful end the previous spring. She and Daddy had their clandestine marriage in July 1936—they probably met shortly after Agnes's birth, around the time Magdi and her family were preparing to leave for Paris. The young man she loved never married and was killed in Auschwitz along with his parents.

I had never heard this story before, but in an odd way it did not surprise me. I had always felt that Mother and Daddy were fundamentally mismatched, despite their sexual harmony. This story struck me as a confirmation. If she had married him on the rebound, still mourning the love she had put all her hopes in, it would explain why she made so little effort to please him during the years of their marriage. In her mind, all she had to do was seduce him; once she was sure of him, she saw no more need to bend to his will (as she may have put it to herself). It did not occur to her that a marriage, and even a passionate love, is an ongoing negotiation, not a onetime deal. She would not cut her hair and wear a shaytl, would not make any effort to overcome her father-in-law's disapproval. A strong-willed woman may go out of her way to please someone she is madly in love with, but not someone she thinks of as only second best. Or so I tell myself.

The story made me understand a little better why she had responded as she did to my breakup with Aaron two years earlier. When she heard that Aaron's parents had advised him to go slower with me, not to head so quickly toward marriage, it must have stirred up old feelings of rejection, of not being found "good enough," and she had blurted them out as was her habit. The more I knew about her, the more I wanted to forgive her.

Almost twenty years after my father died, in the spring of 1978, I was living in Paris during a sabbatical year with my husband and children. Mother, who had remarried a few months earlier after her long widowhood, came to visit us with her new husband—it was her first and only return to Europe. They were on their way to visit his daughter in Israel and stopped off in Paris for a week. I had reserved a room for them in a hotel near our apartment, not far from the Luxembourg Gardens. It was late April and the chestnut trees were in bloom, a perfect time for sightseeing. But Mother was more interested in her grandsons (Michael had just turned eight and Daniel would turn one in a few weeks), so we spent a lot of time indoors, playing Rummikub with Michael and applauding the baby as he crawled on the rug. Mother seemed very happy, in a way I had never seen before. Since my father's death I had gotten used to seeing her always alone, or with her sister; now she was part of a couple, and the idea seemed to delight her. Her husband, a retired Hungarian dentist, liked to tell bad jokes we could not quite make out, since his English was much worse than hers. But he had an appealing manner and he doted on her, I noted with satisfaction. One nice detail in this story, almost poetic in its circularity, is that Mother's new husband, the widower with whom she spent ten happy years before her death, had the same

family name as her first love: Farkas, which means "wolf" in Hungarian. Far from being ferocious, Dr. Farkas was a gentle man who adored my mother. They never fought, for he—unlike my father—did everything she wanted and demanded nothing but her affection in return. Late in life, she had found a husband who was perfect for her.

A few weeks after they left, my husband and I were invited to dinner at the home of a French colleague, Judith, whose family was originally from Hungary. One of the guests, a woman who knew the hostess well but whom we had just met, smiled broadly when she heard my name. "I met your mother," she told me. Really? How? I asked. "Oh, in the street. I was crossing the rue Gay-Lussac a few weeks ago, and I saw a little old couple who didn't seem to know which way to turn. Just the way they were walking, with tiny steps, hanging on to each other, I knew immediately they were Jews from Eastern Europe—they reminded me of Judith's mother. So I asked them if they needed help and led them to their hotel. They were really sweet, invited me for a coffee, and your mother told me about you. She's very proud of you, you know, and of her 'famous son-in-law' too, as she called him, who has published books about French politics. She also told us about your two sons, the eight-year-old who speaks perfect French, and the baby. I know a lot about your family, even though we never met before today!"

Mother, true to her ways, had struck up a conversation with a stranger even in a foreign country. So that was how this young Frenchwoman saw her—a sweet old Jewish lady from Eastern Europe. I never thought of her as old, nor as sweet. Tough, opinionated, anxious, tactless, fiercely attached to life and to her children; but not old, not sweet. You can never tell how a book will be read, even if you wrote it. You can never tell how your children will see you, even if you gave them birth.

12

Round-Trip Tickets

Once back at Barnard, I threw myself into my studies with an intensity I had not experienced since the course on the Faust myth over a year earlier—it was as if the science and math drudgery had never existed. I was admitted to a creative writing class with the then up-and-coming poet Robert Pack, who had a following among aspiring writers in the college (Erica Jong and Rosellen Brown were in the class), and after much labor I produced a sonnet that appeared in the Barnard literary magazine. I also enrolled in a course on modern literature and art, taught by a charismatic professor, Barry Ulanov. I knew little about Professor Ulanov but liked the fact that he had a reputation as "cool." He wrote about jazz for popular magazines, and a jazz musician he knew had even written a song called "Coolin' Off with Ulanov." As I found out later, Barry Ulanov was a deeply religious man, having converted to Catholicism from his native Judaism just a few years earlier. After his retirement from Barnard in the 1980s, he wrote several books from a Catholic perspective; in 1959, however, he appeared to me only as a handsome, magnetic man who was up to date on everything. We read one of Lawrence Durrell's novels in his class just a year after it appeared, proof of Professor Ulanov's coolness. We also read Djuna Barnes's *Nightwood*, written in Paris in the 1930s, a modernist classic that left me cold. If Barnes's somewhat tortuous prose sought to alienate the reader, it achieved its aim perfectly, with no compensatory pleasure in my case. Besides, I was put off by Barnes's apparent scornfulness toward Jews, similar to that of T. S. Eliot (whom we also read, but whose poetry spoke to me). I was no longer religious, but being Jewish still mattered to me, especially in response to antisemitism.

Gertrude Stein was on the syllabus too, as was Virginia Woolf, but we read these women's works with no mention of gender. Barry Ulanov, for all his coolness, was a man of his time. Still, he opened my eyes to comparative study, and he encouraged us to take risks when we wrote about literature and art. Rereading the essays I wrote for his class (yes, I kept them!), I am struck by the confident assertions I made as a twenty-year-old novice critic, evoking Auden's poetry in one breath and Picasso's Blue Period in another.

In addition to the English courses, I began a systematic study of French literature, from the eighteenth century to the twentieth. Someone once asked me, years later, why I had decided to focus on French literature instead of English or American, given that I so very much wanted to be American in those days. The question surprised me, then made me think. Was it the orderliness of French that attracted me, as it had earlier in Vienna and Haiti? Was it my warm memories of our time in Paris, on the way to America? In the end, I decided it was something else. Just as I had left Chicago after high school at the very moment when I could almost think of myself as being fully of that place, so choosing to study French literature may have been a way of not being fully (only "almost") in the place of Americanness. I had left Hungary behind, had been happy to become an American citizen, but Hungary was in Europe, and so was France. If Hungarian had become a mother tongue I could speak only like a fourth-grader, French would become my stepmother tongue, spoken and written with the ease of one who was almost a native, a European. What about English, then? Today it is the language I know best of all, the one I write most spontaneously. If there is such a thing as a faux mother tongue, mine is English.

Deep reasons aside, I liked French literature. I admired Voltaire's irony ("All's well in the best of all possible worlds!"), recited with some irony of my own the Romantic alexandrines of Victor Hugo, and discovered the power of disenchantment in the novels of Balzac and Flaubert. But my true love was for the moderns: Proust and Gide were tutelary figures, outdone only by Sartre and Camus. That was not very original of me, since college students all over the country were swarming to their works. It is hard to exaggerate the glamor that was attached in those days to writers we thought of as having been in the Resistance against Nazism, writers who wrote about the absurdity of the human condition and yet proclaimed the value of existence. "Existentialism is a humanism," Sartre had declared. Life is absurd, but individuals are still free to make choices. We must imagine Sisyphus happy, Camus had concluded in *The Myth of Sisyphus*, his book about why suicide is not a solution to the absurdity of existence. Imagine as happy a man eternally rolling the same stone up the hill, only to watch it fall back when he neared the top? If Camus said it, it must be worth thinking about; maybe what mattered in life was the process, not the victory. When Camus was killed in an absurd automobile accident in January 1960, I and many others went into a kind of mourning.

Sartre had the added prestige of being the male half of an extraordinary couple. Simone de Beauvoir, famous in her own right, was his lover, his best friend, his lifelong partner in intellectual adventure. She had published her coming-of-age memoir, *Memoirs of a Dutiful Daughter*, the year before, and I devoured it even though it was not required reading—very few books by women writers were required reading in 1959, even in a women's college like Barnard. When Beauvoir described how she had met Sartre at the Sorbonne while they were both studying for a difficult competitive examination, and how they later made a pact to be totally committed to each other while remaining free, I dreamed that I too would one day meet a man I could admire and love like that. Much has been written since then about the less-than-perfect relationship between Sartre and Beauvoir, but at the time it seemed ideal.

My dream almost came true with the reappearance of Ted, a Columbia student who had been part of my old boyfriend Alex's circle and had graduated the previous year. He had spent a year traveling around Europe on the cheap, covering reams of paper with the draft of a novel and dozens of poems—but he never bothered to edit what he wrote and had not succeeded in getting his work published. He and his father, a doctor in Brooklyn, had agreed that if he did not publish anything that year, he would return to New York and prepare to apply to medical school. Having been an English major, Ted needed science courses (some of the very ones I had recently left behind), and he returned to Columbia to fulfill that requirement. He seemed to me romantic and brooding, unhappy with his place in the world just as a poet should be. He showed me his poems. I could tell they needed some serious editing, but true poets did not bother with such details, I thought. Did Rimbaud—or closer to home, Allen Ginsberg, who had been a student at Columbia ten years earlier—worry about spelling and punctuation? I began to fall in love with Ted.

We would go for long walks in Riverside Park while he told me about Florence and Barcelona, Rome and Copenhagen, all the cities he had visited the previous year. Some afternoons he would shepherd me onto the subway and we would go down to the White Horse Tavern, the hangout on Hudson Street where the Beat poets had gathered just a few years earlier. Ted had all kinds of theories about poetry, and he expounded them to me as we sat before our glasses of red wine. (I was not twenty-one yet, but he was.) Clearly, he would become a reluctant doctor—but after all, William Carlos Williams had been a doctor, and Wallace Stevens an insurance executive. Even poets had to earn a living.

Ted was the first young man, after Aaron, who excited me physically, and he had the added attraction of eliciting my admiration for his mind. Strangely, we never quite succeeded in becoming a couple. We made various attempts, over the years that followed, to envisage a life together, but in the end, we remained simply lifelong friends. He became a psychiatrist and continued to write poetry, never editing what he wrote—every once in a while, a thick manila envelope would arrive in the mail, containing his latest poems. By then, I had become less tolerant of his sloppiness. I thought he had real talent but not quite enough to get away without doing the hard work that comes after inspiration. Every few months, he would call me and we would talk about his job, his wife, his children. Occasionally, if I happened to be in New York, we would meet for lunch. He remained unhappy and brooding to the end. He died of a heart ailment a few years ago.

Around the middle of spring semester, I suddenly realized that graduation was only a couple of months away and I had no plans for afterward. My father had asked, a few months before his death, "What can you do with literature?" What indeed? As he had told me, I had no safety net—true now more than ever.

I went to talk to the French professor who had taught my

nineteenth-century literature course. Helen Bailey, a kind and motherly woman, was dean of the faculty in addition to being a French professor, and she had taken an interest in me after learning that my father had died just weeks before the start of senior year. I was a good student, she said—had been on the dean's list (an honors list based on grades) every year and would no doubt be elected to Phi Beta Kappa. Why not apply to graduate school and earn a PhD? I explained to her that I had no money. "There are fellowships," she said. For example, the Woodrow Wilson Fellowship Foundation offered to support outstanding seniors throughout their graduate studies, with an aim toward recruiting future college professors. Professor Bailey said she would recommend me if I wanted to apply for it. I would need to fill out some forms, attach my curriculum vitae, explain why I wanted to study French literature. After that, if I made the final cut, I would be interviewed, and if I passed that stage the foundation would fund my studies wherever I wanted. I thanked her and said I would think it over.

I had never prepared a curriculum vitae and wasn't even sure exactly how to spell it (was it *curriculum* or *curriculae*?), but I decided to go ahead and apply. It was already too late for September 1960, so Professor Bailey suggested that I spend a year in Paris and apply from there for the following fall. I spoke French very well, she said, but I could use some advanced training in grammar and pronunciation. Paris would be good for me, she added—I was not sure exactly what she meant by that, but I trusted her. Besides, I still remembered our enchanted weeks there on our way to Haiti. She would recommend me for a small traveling scholarship from Barnard, she said, which would at least be a start.

Travel to Paris as an American college graduate, not as a Hungarian refugee? Once the thought had been planted in my mind, I could not stop thinking about it. I had spent so many years and so much effort becoming American—would a return to Europe undermine my Americanness? Or, on the contrary, would it affirm it? I would be traveling with an American passport, like any number of young men and women from all over the country, looking to Europe for culture and discovery. I thought of all the famous writers who had gone to Paris from America: Gertrude Stein, Ernest Hemingway, F. Scott Fitzgerald, Henry Miller, and before them Edith Wharton, Henry James. Maybe I too could become a writer. Hadn't I published a sonnet in the Barnard literary magazine?

In September 1960, I boarded the *SS Flandres* in New York and arrived in London a week later. I was back in Europe, almost exactly ten years after I had made the journey away from it with my parents. Now I was on my own, an American college graduate on a stopover in London, bound for a year of postgraduate study in Paris. I owed that crucial year to Barnard and to my Uncle Nick, who had once again become a hero in my tale by offering me a modest monthly stipend abroad as a graduation present. Henceforth, my life would be defined by round trips between Europe and America, not one-way tickets.

Upon arrival in Paris, my head full of Sartre and Beauvoir, who had spent many years living in cheap hotels on the Left Bank before becoming famous, I rented a sixth-floor walk-up in a hotel on the rue Delambre in Montparnasse, around the corner from Le Dôme and La Rotonde, cafés I had read about in Beauvoir's memoirs. Montparnasse had been an artistic mecca already before World War I, when Modigliani and Chagall walked those streets; by 1960, the avant-garde had moved on, but the neighborhood retained its artistic glamor. Sartre and Beauvoir both lived in the neighborhood, although I never caught a glimpse of them

The Grand Hotel des Bains, as its name implied, housed a public bath in its courtyard—apartments in Paris often still had nothing more than a sink and a toilet in those days (just like Aunt Magdi's and Uncle Béla's place ten years earlier), their inhabitants bathing in a public bath once a week. One thing about the hotel I found out only after moving in was that many guests rented rooms by the hour—the sounds of sex were unmistakable through the paper-thin walls. In my search for the bohemian life, I had landed in an *hôtel de passe*, where the prostitutes who roamed the neighborhood took their clients (*passe* is French slang for a prostitute's "quickie"). They and the forty-watt bulbs in the ceiling lights, the only lighting in the room, made reading and writing somewhat difficult. I was still nurturing the idea of becoming a writer and had begun a novel about a young woman in New York and Paris that never got beyond the first chapter. In late October, when the cold weather started, I realized that the room was not heated as I lay shivering under the thin blanket. Admitting defeat, I applied for lodging in the Pavillon des États-Unis, the American dormitory at the Cité Universitaire, the large student complex near the Porte d'Orléans in the south of Paris; it was only a few subway stops from Montparnasse.

I was assigned a large double room, sharing it with a petite Vietnamese student whose slender figure I envied. We had all the heat we needed, good lighting, and hot showers available in the hall near our room. But I was not happy, being completely at sea about my plans for the future. What would I do, once my year in Paris was over? I had applied for a Woodrow Wilson Fellowship but was still awaiting the result. Meanwhile, I attended classes at the Sorbonne in advanced French grammar, taught by a talented instructor named Madame Stourdzé, who could make even the imperfect subjunctive a compelling subject, and in phonetics, which revealed the mysteries of French vowels (*é*

versus *è, eu* versus *oeu, a* versus *â*), finally allowing me to speak
French almost like a native.

But mainly, I lay on my bed and read. Over that whole
winter, I read the volumes of Proust I hadn't read in college,
everything after *Swann's Way*. My roommate got worried about
me as I lay there day after day without moving, just turning the
pages. Proust dazzled me, not the same way that Thomas Mann
had a few years earlier, but unforgettably. His understanding of
the vagaries of human behavior and psychology (the way we lie
to ourselves, for example, like the friend of the Narrator's family
who is always railing against snobs but turns out to be the biggest snob himself, or like the Duc de Guermantes, who claims
to be in too much of a hurry to an important appointment to
pay proper attention to his friend Swann's announcement that
he is dying, but then orders his wife the duchess to go upstairs
and change her shoes, lateness be damned, for one simply cannot go out wearing the wrong color shoes) struck me as wise
to the point of prophetic insight. Everyone thinks of Proust
as the great theorist of memory, and he was that too, but as I
lay there in my dorm room in Paris, devouring the pages of *In
Search of Lost Time*, it was his superb observations about people
in social interactions that enthralled me. At a party when he is
just slightly acquainted with the Duchesse de Guermantes, who
would later become his friend, the Narrator rises considerably in
her esteem when, instead of brashly running up to her to greet
her, he merely nods to her from a distance. Thus does adher-
ence to the unwritten rules of polite society acquire an almost
moral dimension—at least in the eyes of the duchess, whom the
Narrator both admires and mercilessly lampoons. How I loved
literature, which can become a guide to life itself!

Sometime in January, I saw a notice on the bulletin board of the American House: a French student was offering *"promenades à Paris"* in exchange for English conversation. The idea appealed to me, and I called his number. That was the beginning of my story with Lucien de L., whose name out of a novel by Balzac or Stendhal added to his appeal. Though not particularly handsome, Lucien was attractive enough: tall, with wavy black hair, wearing glasses, he was studying economics at Sciences Po, the prestigious Institute for Political Science. We met every week for a long walk around Paris, about which he knew a great deal. He showed me the Conciergerie, the tower on the Seine where Marie Antoinette had been imprisoned before being beheaded, and other historic sites. But I didn't keep my part of the bargain, because we spoke only in French.

Often, at the end of our walk, we would sit in a café and talk about our lives. He was an only child, lived with his widowed mother in St. Cloud, a fashionable suburb. While his family was Catholic, he told me, he himself didn't go to church. He knew that I was Jewish, and I told him about my own widowed mother and little sister, who were living in Miami Beach by then. After a month or two, he invited me to Sunday lunch in St. Cloud and introduced me to his mother, a blond lady who greeted me graciously. Despite their aristocratic name and their house and garden, my impression was that they were not wealthy—not at all unusual for aristocratic families in France at that time. Lucien was studying economics so that he could become rich, I often thought. He had a very practical, not at all romantic view of life.

A couple of weeks after my visit to St. Cloud, in the middle of one of our walks, Lucien brought me to a sudden halt by asking me to marry him. This was so unexpected that I could only gape at him—we had never once kissed, we shook hands when we met and parted, and said *vous* to each other instead of the familiar *tu*. But he was serious, he insisted. He had wanted his mother to meet me and she had liked me. He wanted to marry me. I thanked him and said I would think about it, then went back to my dorm to puzzle over it. Was this how aristocrats did things? I wondered. Proust was no help here. Finally, my cynicism won out and I decided that Lucien must think I'm a rich American girl, a perfect match for an impoverished but ambitious young French nobleman. There was no other plausible explanation, I thought. It amused me, since rich was very far from what I was. When I saw him again the following week, I told him gently but firmly that I was not ready to be married, even though I was quite fond of him. He looked crushed. That was the end of our walks around Paris.

Many months later, when I was visiting her from Cambridge, Mother gave me a letter that had arrived for me in Miami Beach—it was from Lucien. I must have given him my address at some point during our walks. I no longer recall what the letter said, exactly, but I think it was a love letter of sorts. Looking back on it, I wonder why it had never occurred to me that he might be genuinely in love with me. Did I feel unworthy of being loved? Maybe it was a more general lack of trust in people—or else I had read too many novels by Balzac, the ultimate disenchanter where love and money are concerned. (*Eugénie Grandet*, about a provincial heiress whose money is what attracts the man she falls in love with and who ultimately abandons her, is a good example—I had read it in college.)

When spring rolled around, I decided I had to earn some money. Uncle Nick's monthly checks took care of subsistence living, and I was grateful for them, but I was yearning for some of the luxuries Paris had to offer. In those days, women, even students at the Sorbonne, still took great care to dress when they went out (jeans and sensible shoes, today's uniform among many professional women in Paris, were far down the horizon), and I often noticed their silk scarves and beautifully tailored skirts. On my walks with Lucien, we had passed many designer boutiques near the Place de la Concorde, along the very elegant rue du Faubourg St. Honoré. Chanel and Dior were out of the question, but one day as I was walking in that neighborhood I noticed a navy blue suit in a more modest window. It had a short skirt and a jacket with a soft collar, and the blue was not dark navy but a more springlike hue, between navy and royal. On an impulse, I went in and asked to try it on. In Paris, one does not enter a boutique lightly, even today. The moment you set your foot in, a chicly dressed saleslady appears, and she'll rarely let you go without trying to convince you that you simply must have whatever item caught your fancy. Or if not that one, then something else. As it turned out, the suit was perfect for me. The size in the window was too small, but I could tell even so that the jacket was flattering. *"C'est parfait, mademoiselle,"* gushed the saleslady, assuring me that they would make one to my size and have it ready in less than a month—with a fitting in between, of course.

I had almost nothing left of that month's check, but I gave her a small deposit, with the promise to settle the bill at the fitting. Then I set about seriously looking for a part-time job. That turned out to be quite easy, because I had a skill that businessmen in France were just beginning to realize they needed to acquire: I knew English. I headed over to the Berlitz school near the Avenue de l'Opéra and was hired immediately, even though I had not the slightest experience teaching anything, let alone English as a second language. These days, teaching ESL is a full-fledged field of specialization, but back then it was enough if you were a native speaker. I was not even that, but my accent was so slight that very few people noticed it, certainly not the lady who interviewed me. The way the school worked, she explained, was that in addition to lessons offered in their offices, they sent teachers out to *entreprises*, businesses where executives could take group lessons without having to spend time traveling. Starting the following week, I made a weekly trip to a factory in a northern suburb, Gennevilliers, accessible by a long metro ride followed by a fifteen-minute walk. My class consisted of about twenty men, midlevel middle-aged executives. I dutifully prepared my lessons and we went through the book provided by Berlitz. After class, one of the men would drive me to the metro stop for the trip back to the dorm. Apparently the lessons went well, because at the end of June, when I was getting ready to leave Paris, my class gave me a going-away present and we ended our last session with a *pot*, a glass of wine. They all toasted me and wished me well, and then my usual driver took me to the metro.

In the meantime, I had picked up my elegant new suit and had even bought a matching *tricot*, a lightweight pullover that the saleslady assured me would be perfect with it. I wore that suit for several years, always with immense pleasure, whenever I wanted to look "Parisian." I put it on the first opportunity I had when I returned to the States, where Mother and Aunt Magdi pronounced that it was a truly chic outfit. Coming from Aunt Magdi, that was immense praise, because she had lived for many years in Paris before and after the war and was considered an expert in such matters. I had always had a special fondness for her, not least because of her Paris connection.

Sylvia B., who had been one of the first people I met when I arrived in Paris, was the aunt of my former boyfriend Alex in New York. Just as Alex was the first person in his Brooklyn family to go to college, so Sylvia, his father's sister, was the first and only artist, an even greater anomaly in that solidly lower middle-class Jewish clan—especially so for a woman. Alex admired her greatly and urged me to look her up when I got to Paris, where she had been living for many years. He had given me her phone number and I called her while I was still living in my hotel room; when she heard I was a friend of her nephew, she invited me to tea.

Sylvia lived on the rue de Seine, not far from the river, in an ancient building with a winding set of stairs; her studio was on the top floor, and as I climbed I noticed the indentations that centuries of walkers had created in the stone steps. The woman who opened the door was striking, around forty years old, with beautiful, deep-set eyes and dark hair pulled back from her forehead. She wore a simple, well-tailored dress and large gold earrings—a woman of the world, I thought. Next to her I felt terribly awkward, but she put me at ease and was soon asking me questions in a friendly way. What did I hope to achieve during my year in Paris? I told her I wasn't sure but hoped things would become clear as the year progressed. "Yes, Paris has a knack for letting you know who you are," she said, but one must learn its ways. For example, I should get a good haircut because looks mattered, even if you were an artist or an intellectual. The next day, I went and did as she said.

I wondered where she did her painting, for I didn't see an easel around. But she soon gave me a tour of her studio and showed me the curtained-off area where she worked. I could see a few abstract paintings in pastel colors leaning against the wall. Beautiful light poured in from the tall windows—she loved her studio, she said. She had bought it with the money she made doing fashion illustrations for a big department store, as her paintings alone could not have supported her. I asked her when she had decided to become an artist. "Oh, I started drawing when I was a kid and never stopped," she laughed. She was a terrible student, drawing all over her schoolbooks, but then went on to the Parsons School of Design, which she liked. After graduation, she worked as a waitress during the day and painted at night; she had first visited Paris right after the war and had been bowled over by the fantastic sense of freedom she experienced there. In 1950, she moved to Paris for good and never looked back, she concluded.

Over the following months, I saw Sylvia several times, and she was always ready to dispense good advice about the ways of Paris. When I went on a skiing trip in December, she lent me the necessary clothes. One day, as we were walking near her house, we bumped into a tall, distinguished-looking man who turned out to be the fashion designer Hubert de Givenchy. He greeted her warmly, with a kiss on both cheeks—I was very impressed: she really was a woman of the world, I told myself. But despite her worldliness, she was also genuinely committed to her work as an artist, and a few years ago I found an interview with her on YouTube when she was ninety years old, having gained a certain small celebrity at a time when women artists were finding more of an audience for their work. In the interview she never mentions a companion or husband, but I think she was living with a man when I knew her. Still, she came across as very much of an independent woman and that was what I admired in her.

It's quite characteristic of me, unfortunately, that I did not keep up the friendship with Sylvia after I left Paris and started graduate school. We moved in different worlds, mine being a lot more conventional and academic than hers. Part of her prestige in my eyes was that she lived what I thought of as an artistic life, which I saw as no contradiction with her worldliness. I too had dreamed of such a life when I first got to Paris, but my few weeks in the *hôtel de passe* had been enough to send me scurrying for safety and comfort in the university dorms. I was willing to take risks in some aspects of my life (going on an

expert skiing trip when I had never been on skis, for example),
but I obviously wanted security. I suppose my lack of money,
my experience as an immigrant, and the early loss of my father
contributed to my sense that a steady salary was essential. When
I was notified, in the spring, that I had been awarded a Woodrow
Wilson Fellowship, I jumped at the opportunity to start graduate
studies at Harvard, which would lead to a teaching position in
a college or university.

Around April 1961, a small bomb went off in the Pavillon des
États-Unis, where I lived; luckily, it didn't hurt anyone and did
only minor damage. It was part of the generally tense climate
that year over the war in Algeria, which was heading toward
its end. The previous September, a number of famous writers
and intellectuals had published the "Manifesto of the 121,"
which called on French soldiers to refuse to serve in Algeria;
in retaliation, members of "Algérie Française" groups, which
opposed Algerian independence, set off bombs all over the city,
including one in front of Jean-Paul Sartre's apartment. It was
not clear who had bombed the American House, or why, since
the U.S. was not involved in Algeria (it was too early to be
an anti–Vietnam War action). Since I was quite apolitical at
the time, to me the bombing was no more than a temporary
diversion.

Looking back on that year now, I am aware of just how
many other things passed me by. For example, I was totally
uninterested in, and therefore unaware of, Jewish survivors of
World War II and the Holocaust, yet Paris was full of them,
including many who had been children like me. The person I
am now would have been thrilled at the opportunity to meet
them, but I was not the same person then. Proust is brilliant
about things like this, showing how people can sometimes no

longer recognize their younger selves. "Was that really me, the young woman so indifferent to a subject of enormous interest to me now?" Or, on the contrary: "How could I have spent years of my life suffering over my love for a woman who was not even my type?" That is the question Swann asks himself after he has fallen out of love with Odette, but when he was still in love with her, he could think of nothing else but her.

Do we become strangers to ourselves as our life moves on? The preceding examples seem to suggest that, yet I also have a strong sense of possessing the same inner self as when I was ten years old. That is the mystery: how we can grow and change to the point of feeling like someone else, and also feel exactly the same, the one and only selfsame being that we refer to throughout our life as "I."

A framed black-and-white photograph sits on a bookshelf in my study: a portrait of a young woman with a pale face and sad eyes, her head slightly tilted, the suggestion of a smile playing about her lips. She wears a dark sweater matching the darkness of her hair, which frames her face in a short bob. No necklace, no earrings. She is striking, with a wistfulness in her expression that could call to mind an ingenue in a 1950s movie. The photo is of me, taken by a professional photographer—I vaguely remember needing an official photo for some French documents, and this must have been it. It was taken in Paris in the fall of 1960 or early 1961, when I was asking myself what to do with my life. But the sad eyes go back to a far earlier time; they remind me of the little girl in the light blue wool dress, posing for the photographer in Budapest after the departures of her loved ones, or of the college student sitting on a bench on Lake Michigan, trying to comfort herself with poetry.

In Paris that year, I felt truly alone. Yes, I met other students, had a mentor of sorts and role model in Sylvia, even a couple of boyfriends. Back home I had a mother, a sister, uncles and aunts who loved me. But the father I adored, who had

 taught me to play chess and drive a car, to make drinking water from fresh snow while bombs were falling, and who had modeled for me a life devoted to learning and striving against odds, was gone. Death is forever. For the rest of my life, I would be a woman without a father. A woman who had to stand on her own.

It was many years before I returned to Budapest, my starting point. Meanwhile, I learned to close doors behind me. Departures at dawn, at noon, at dusk, with someone beside me or more often alone. *Don't forget to leave the key.* Departures between anticipation and regret, even if I always had a home address. (But what is a home you are always leaving?) So many faces never to be seen again.

Today, Budapest is one more city I know—but it is where my memories began. Along with Paris, it is a place of arrivals as well as departures. A place I love, but not my home.

And America? How could I not love it too? It is the place where I became who I am, where my children and grandchildren were born and live, the place where my parents are buried and where I will be buried when my time comes. It is the place of my home address. I would be lying if I said I feel fully American—but why should we be fully anything? Incompleteness is the human lot.

Between cities, between cultures, never feeling that I totally belong but not an outcast either. That place of self-division—not exactly a fracture, but not quite a plenitude—is where I feel at home.

Epilogue

"But what about later?" a friend complains. She wants me to write more about my career, how I wound up getting tenure at Harvard when it was still a relative rarity for a woman. About my children, my marriage, about all the struggles along the way.

That would be a whole other book. In this one, I have wanted to explore how I became the woman I am, and I believe the process was largely complete by the time I returned from my year in Paris. Still, I once wrote that we are not only the children of our parents, that history too nourishes us or deprives us of nourishment; James Baldwin expressed a similar idea when he asserted that "history is literally *present* in all that we do."[1] If I take these ideas seriously—and I hope this book has demonstrated that I do—then I should at least try to reflect on how my career was influenced by the larger historical movements that accompanied it.

Here is an anecdote. In the fall of 1965, now a Harvard graduate student working on my dissertation, I was back in Paris to do research. My days consisted largely of sitting and taking

---

1. "White Man's Guilt," in *The Price of the Ticket: Collected Nonfiction 1948-1985* (Boston: Beacon Press, 1985), 414.

notes in the grand Reading Room of the National Library on the rue de Richelieu, surrounded by scholars intent on their own work. It was a monotonous existence, mainly, but one I found extremely satisfying as my notes piled up. I had made some friends among the other researchers, French and American, whom I would meet for a break in the café on the square across the way every afternoon. One day I left the library a bit earlier than usual to attend a lecture by a Harvard professor I knew, Laurence Wylie, who had recently been appointed as cultural attaché at the American embassy—a temporary position often occupied by a distinguished academic. The event took place in French, at the Institute for Political Science on the Left Bank. After the lecture, the floor was open for questions and I eventually asked one. I can no longer remember what I said, but it was based on some of the reading I had been doing (my dissertation was about a "committed" novelist of the 1930s, very involved in politics) and I spoke animatedly for a few minutes. Afterward, I went up and said hello to Professor Wylie, who was surrounded by important people but took the time to greet me. Then I left.

The next morning, I received a phone call at the student dorm where I was living. "This is Bert Leefmans," the caller said. "I am the chair of the undergraduate French department at Columbia University and I heard you at Larry Wylie's talk yesterday, then saw you speak to him afterward. He gave me your name. Can we meet? I'd like to offer you a job." I tried not to show how flabbergasted I felt. We made an appointment for later that week, and Bert Leefmans explained that an instructorship in French was available in Columbia College, the Ivy League men's college of Columbia University. He was in Paris on sabbatical, but he would inform the colleague in New York who was temporarily replacing him and I could start as early as February. But I didn't have my PhD yet, I told him. It didn't matter, the instructorship didn't require a doctorate, he said. It was non–tenure track, not an assistant professorship, but still a full-time job teaching French language and literature in a prestigious men's college. The annual contract was renewable for up to five years.

Since I was planning to get married in New York in February, to a young man I had met at Harvard who was doing his graduate work in political science at Columbia, the offer seemed providential. It never occurred to me to ask how Bert Leefmans could simply offer me a job without consulting anyone back on campus. Nowadays, even a low-level teaching position would have to be advertised, with several candidates interviewed by a committee that would make the decision. Back then, the chair could decide on his own. It was entirely to Bert Leefman's credit that he offered the job to a woman; there were no other women instructors at the time at Columbia College.

When I arrived in New York in December, I went to see the acting chair of the department, who was expecting me with papers to sign. We conversed in French, his native language, and he seemed satisfied with my command of it. He told me about the courses I would teach and emphasized that I would be the first full-time woman instructor at the college. Since I had already done some teaching as part of my graduate studies, I felt no qualms about the assignment, but I sensed that he was looking at me with some suspicion, or skepticism, as if he was not totally happy with this new hire that had been foisted on him. His colleague Leefmans could at least have consulted him before making the offer, instead of merely informing him about it! Or maybe he was just having a bad day. At any rate, before we parted, he said, with a smile that he may have intended to be friendly but that I interpreted as a smirk, *"Vous comprenez, il n'y a pas d'avenir ici pour vous." You understand, there is no future here for you.* Oh, I understood perfectly, I assured him—I had no illusions about a future here but was glad to be hired for a few years.

That is how things were in academic life, back in 1965. It was not impossible for a woman instructor to be hired by an Ivy League institution, but it required the will of a powerful man to accomplish it. Had a committee been doing the hiring, I would probably not have been selected, but Bert Leefmans, acting on an impulse, took the risk. His colleague, however, felt no compunction about reminding me that I should keep my expectations low. I cannot imagine such a bare-facedly sexist statement being made out loud (though no doubt the private sentiment was still widely shared) a mere half dozen years later, after the political upheavals of 1968 and the start of the women's movement.

As it turned out, I did not have much of a future at Columbia College, but I did get hired as an assistant professor in 1969, after obtaining my doctorate. There were now two young women assistant professors of French at Columbia: Naomi Schor, who became a lifelong friend, was hired fresh out of her graduate studies at Yale the same year. We did not exactly constitute a cohort, and I was too busy with my obligations as a wife and mother to spend much time in socializing, but at least I was no longer the only woman in the room.

My son Michael was born in April 1970, on a day when I had taught a class in the morning. No college or university in those years had a policy of family or maternity leave—I was back in the classroom within two weeks after giving birth, having barely had a chance to become acquainted with my beautiful baby boy, named after my father. In early May, when the Ohio National Guard fired on anti-Vietnam demonstrators at Kent State University, killing four students, Columbia and many other universities shut down and I met my students in my apartment. It was a kind of improvised leave, courtesy of History.

Although Columbia was not very accommodating to women faculty, my years there were not wasted. I benefited greatly from the intellectual ferment that was going on in French studies during those years, when Columbia was constantly hosting lectures by the latest messsengers from France. New theories about literature and society were crossing the Atlantic at a steady pace: structuralism, deconstruction, Lacanian psychoanalysis, and "French feminism" all arrived in New York within a few years of each other. I felt as if I were back in graduate school, learning something new every day. Harvard had not been in the forefront of welcoming new movements when I was a student there, so this was a brand-new education for me. It was intellectually exciting and physically exhausting to run from home to class to the latest lecture, even while making sure that Michael was taken care of and dinner was cooked. My husband and I both had small salaries as assistant professors (he was teaching at the City University of New York), so there was no question of hiring a full-time nanny. It was around that time that I began to think seriously about a subject I would write about extensively a few years later: the pressures, both external and internal, that women face (I use the present tense because it is still true) if they try to combine motherhood and marriage with a demanding career—in my case, teaching and writing. Marriage and motherhood demand long hours of presence to the needs of another person; writing demands long hours of intense work alone. I did not have many long hours of either kind available to me, and to this day women in academia and other professions struggle with those demands.

Neither Naomi Schor nor I obtained tenure when it came time for that, in 1975. Naomi had published her dissertation as a book, which was considered the sine qua non for tenure, but she was denied it anyway. I had not published my dissertation, so I had less to complain about—but I had edited a book and published a few articles, including a substantial one in a prestigious French journal. Engaging with the latest critical theories but breaking new ground, that article became the basis of the book that earned me tenure at Harvard some years later. Naomi went on to a brilliant career as a professor of nineteenth-century French literature, and we often joked about how neither of us had made the grade the first time. Her premature death in 2001 was a real loss, both to me personally and to our profession.

In 1974, my husband, Ezra Suleiman, a political scientist specializing in France, accepted a tenured professorship at UCLA, and we had a commuting marriage while I waited for the tenure decision at Columbia. Michael and I stayed in New York while Ezra flew in from Los Angeles every couple of weeks. Commuting marriages were a fairly new thing at the time, and we were both interviewed by a woman who was writing a book on the subject. After the axe fell, Michael and I joined Ezra in Los Angeles and within a few months I obtained a tenure-track position at Occidental College, a small liberal arts college which prided itself on the quality of its undergraduate teaching. When I started at Oxy, as it was affectionately called, I was pregnant with my second child, Daniel, who was born in May 1977. By then, I was able to negotiate a few weeks' leave until the end of the school year, which allowed me not to give birth just hours after leaving the classroom and to experience the joy of participating in my baby's first months of life with no competing pressures.

Occidental was a haven of democracy after the hierarchical system that had been in place at Columbia. At Columbia, assistant professors could not make long-distance phone calls from their office, which they shared with several others; at Occidental, not only did everyone have an individual office with long-distance calling capability, but a pool of typists was available to type our manuscripts. (Yes, there was a time before laptops!) I felt, for the first time, fully appreciated and respected as a faculty member, even though I was not yet a tenured professor. I also encountered, for the first time, a community of women scholars deeply involved with their work and interested in the burgeoning field of feminist criticism. In 1976, when I joined the faculty, Occidental had a sizable number of women teaching in a wide variety of fields, from history and politics to film studies and literature. A colleague in my department, Annabelle Rea, who had been at the college for many years, took on the task of acting as my mentor, introducing me to other colleagues and generally smoothing my way; we have remained lifelong friends. A group of women faculty, including Annabelle and me, formed a study group that fostered intellectual exchange while also providing a supportive environment and a form of "consciousness raising." I had not had time to join any feminist groups in New York, but California's more relaxed atmosphere allowed for it. Plus, my family had a higher income, due to my husband's salary as a tenured professor; we hired a student as an au pair to help with child care, and eventually, for a time, a housekeeper.

When I first met him, Ezra was an undergraduate at Harvard, two years younger than I. A Jewish immigrant like me but different from me in every other respect, he was the cherished older son in an extended Sephardic family that had lived for many generations in the city of Basra, in Iraq. His father, Nassim, a businessman with a law degree, had many Arab friends and was versed in the Qur'an—he considered himself both a Jew and a loyal Iraqi, just like the European Jews who had thought of themselves as good Germans or Hungarians in addition to being Jewish. Ezra's mother Sophie was from a similarly prosperous Basra family; she married Nassim at age eighteen and they had five children in quick succession.

Despite some violent antisemitic incidents in 1941, the Suleiman family felt comfortably established in Basra, as did the large Jewish community in Baghdad. After the creation of Israel, however, and the wars that accompanied it (Iraq fought with the Arab League against Israel), the situation of Iraqi Jews changed dramatically. A prominent Jewish businessman in Basra was hanged as a "Zionist spy" in 1948, and over the following years almost all of Iraq's Jews left the country. Many of Ezra's relatives eventually settled in Israel, but Nassim Suleiman chose to stay. He began sending his children abroad to safety, however. Ezra and two of his sisters were sent to boarding school in England in 1950, all of them under the age of ten; their father flew to visit them a few times, but they didn't see their mother again until four years later, when Ezra recalled not recognizing her. After the Suez crisis of 1956 brought more instability to the region, Nassim sent his two youngest children to live with an uncle in the United States, where their mother joined them two years later. Nassim too was planning to leave by then, but the political revolution of July 1958 (which overthrew King Faisal, in power since he was a boy in the 1930s) made leaving impossible. Nassim was jailed for several months and was finally allowed to leave in 1960 with the help of an influential Arab friend. The family settled in Evanston, Illinois, and Nassim became a respected member of the Chicago Board of Trade.

By then, Ezra was at Harvard. We met not long after I arrived there in the fall of 1961 and became romantically involved around the time of his graduation in 1963. We married when I started teaching at Columbia three years later.

The first year of my son Daniel's life was one of the happiest in my life. Ezra and I both had work to do in Paris (our shared love of France was a strong bond between us), and we spent the academic year there, on leave from UCLA and Occidental. Through friends, we found a spacious apartment to rent on the Boulevard St. Michel, a stone's throw from the Luxembourg Gardens. Like many large Parisian apartments, this one had a maid's room on the top floor, normally inhabited by students. A young American woman who had answered our ad for an au pair took care of Daniel for several hours each day, in exchange for the room; she also picked up Michael from school on most afternoons—he was attending second grade, and within a few months had acquired a native accent in French that he still maintains with pride. Karen, our au pair, was friendly and efficient, and she and the baby bonded nicely. Every morning, after I had bathed him and played with him and put him down for his nap, I would retreat to my desk in the room next door, whose windows overlooked the trees in the courtyard. I was writing a long essay for a book of literary theory I was co-editing, *The Reader in the Text*, which later turned out to be a pioneering work. But right now, I simply had the pleasure of being totally engrossed in a task I found compelling, secure in the knowledge that my kids were being taken care of while I wrote.

Karen would arrive in time to pick Daniel up from his nap and feed him lunch, then bundle him into his carriage and take him to the Luxembourg Gardens. In the late afternoon, she would return with the two boys and I would take over for the rest of the day. The daily rhythm, rarely broken, allowed for great progress in my work, as well as for a largely peaceful family life. When Ezra and I went out for the evening, Karen would babysit; when we invited friends to dinner, usually on the weekend, it would become an elaborate production, but one we enjoyed tremendously. How can you fail to love shopping for food, when you have dozens of fabulous cheeses to choose from and a butcher who can tell you exactly how to cook rabbit in mustard sauce?

It was during that year that my mother came to visit us with her new husband, her only return to Europe since 1950. It was also during that year that serious cracks began to show in our marriage. In a sense, everything should have brought us together. We had both suffered separation from our parents as young children, buffeted by historical disasters; we had both switched languages at an early age, both immigrated to the United States (Ezra at a later age than I, so he never had the same drive to assimilate that I did), and both ended up earning PhDs in preparation for teaching and research about France. Unfortunately for our marriage, our similar life stories and career paths may have acted more as obstacles than as vehicles for intimacy and mutual understanding. People with similar emotional baggage are not necessarily able to satisfy each other's needs. If you add to that the conflicting pressures of family life and intellectual and professional ambition, the result can be a great deal of frustration and unhappiness.

That year, neither Ezra nor I heeded the warning signs; on the contrary, we tried to ignore them. In the summer we rented a house near Aix-en-Provence for a month and watched proudly as Michael learned to swim at the local pool while Daniel took his first steps and learned to wave and say "*Au revoir*" to the lifeguards as his father picked him up and carried him home.

When we returned to Los Angeles in the fall, we resumed our teaching and I felt safely on my way to tenure at Occidental. Then a bombshell struck: Ezra, who had published an important book based on his dissertation a few years earlier and then another one right after we returned from Paris, was offered a tenured professorship at Princeton University. It was one of those offers you can't refuse, we both realized, even while recognizing that it would put my own career into jeopardy. Academic jobs in the humanities had become quite scarce in the late 1970s, and many PhDs in literature or philosophy were converting their degrees into executive positions in business or in nonprofit foundations. It was not at all certain that I would be able to get a teaching job on the East Coast, especially as I was between ranks—not yet ready for tenure, but too experienced for an entry-level assistant professorship. We pretended for a few weeks to seriously consider turning down the Princeton offer, but I knew very well I couldn't ask Ezra to make that sacrifice. Besides, we had enjoyed living on the East Coast, and it was a lot closer to France. He accepted.

As we might have foreseen, the decision to move again, with the upheavals it entailed, brought all the hitherto ignored cracks in our marriage to the fore. By the time we arrived in Princeton in the fall of 1979, we were a family in trouble. The next two years brought more unhappiness than I had ever known. The only thing that kept me going was my work, which was actually starting to flourish. The writer's block I had suffered from on and off a few years earlier seemed to be lifted, I had published several articles in major journals, the edited book I had been working on in Paris was about to appear, and the long-delayed book based on "French theory" that I had started to write while at Columbia was finally approaching its end. I was awarded a coveted yearlong fellowship by the National Endowment for the Humanities, which allowed me to do the necessary writing and feel that I was not unemployed in Princeton. I was even acquiring a reputation as an up-and-coming literary theorist and was invited to speak at conferences in the United States and abroad.

There was still no teaching job in the offing, however. After the fellowship ended, I decided to return to California for at least a few months, to reclaim my teaching position and obtain tenure at Occidental. With my marriage on the rocks, I felt I had to have something certain to rely on. Was this a legacy of my chaotic childhood? Surely.

Then, shortly after I had returned to California, in January 1981, Harvard offered me a position as an associate professor. The Department of Romance Languages had invited me to give a lecture there a few weeks earlier, but I was unaware that they were considering me seriously for a job. The offer was not for a tenured position: while at most universities an associate professorship comes with tenure, at Harvard and a few others, only full professors have that permanence—it's an all-or-nothing game, as I have often said to myself. Still, the position was attractive, and the chair of the department, Jules Brody, himself a relative newcomer to Harvard, assured me that just as soon as my "big book" appeared, they would recommend me for tenure.

By then it was too late to cancel Occidental, since classes had already started; in any case, I still wanted to be promoted there. Every other week, I would take the red-eye special from LAX to Newark on Thursday evening and return on Monday morning. Each time I left our house, looking at my sons' sad faces, my eyes filled with tears and I reproached myself for being a bad mother. In a way, I was re-creating for them the trauma of separation I had suffered as a child. I too was suffering, from the pain of separation and from remorse. But I gritted my teeth and went on. I was a survivor, after all.

Occidental awarded me tenure that spring. When I told the dean, Bob Ryf, that I had meanwhile received an offer from Harvard, he asked: "Is it a tenured position?" No, I said, but tenure was promised. "You never know with these big places. Accept the position, but don't resign yet from Oxy," he advised. I never did officially resign from Occidental. (Dear Bob Ryf, I'll never forget your kindness and humanity, at a time when I was hurting so much.)

While the dean was right and nothing was certain, Harvard did award me tenure in 1983, shortly after my book *Authoritarian Fictions: The Ideological Novel as a Literary Genre* was published in France and the United States. I remained on the Harvard faculty for more than three decades. Over the many years I taught there, I also gave lectures and attended conferences all over the world, like the globe-trotting professors in David Lodge's delightful novel, *Small World*. The British novelist Margaret Drabble, when asked how she juggled career and family, replied that at any one time she could do two out of three—career, marriage, motherhood—but not all three. That seemed to be my case as well: after my divorce, I never remarried. Motherhood, however, is permanent; even better, so is grandmotherhood, which has brought me joys I would not trade for anything.

I became known as a literary theorist in the heyday of structuralism and poststructuralism, a feminist critic a few years later, and a specialist in memory of World War II and the Holocaust a few years after that. The truly privileged thing about being a university professor is that you get to teach and write on all the subjects you want to learn about. My career evolved with my passions, and I am very grateful for it.

Among the many artists and writers I admire and have written about is the British Surrealist Leonora Carrington, who lived from 1917 to 2011. She was mainly a painter and occasional sculptor, but she also wrote some wonderfully offbeat stories and novels, of which my favorite is *The Hearing Trumpet*. (I devoted a long chapter to it in my book *Subversive Intent*.) Although Carrington was in her early thirties when she wrote that novel, her heroine is a very old, very deaf, quite daffy lady who becomes the leader of a revolution in her old-age home. Carrington clearly loved her heroine's unruliness, and so did I. Now that I too am an old woman, as my mirror informs me every morning (though not yet deaf, and I hope not too daffy),

I offer you in parting, dear reader, my *Song of the Unruly Old Woman*:

> I am an old woman.
>
> An old woman is not supposed to feel like a young woman, ambivalent toward her mother, guilty at not having loved her enough.
>
> An old woman is not supposed to work, even if she has worked all her life; she should enjoy retirement, take cruises, spend time with the grandchildren.
>
> An old woman is not supposed to sit for hours at her desk, struggling to find the right words; she should realize that her memories are of no interest to anyone but her family and friends, if she is lucky.
>
> An old woman is not supposed to dance.
>
> But what if some rules exist to be broken?
>
> What if old age is a time of freedom?

Acknowledgments

Somewhat perversely, I could thank the COVID virus for forcing me to sit still during the two years it took to write this book. But I won't do that. Instead, I want to thank the friends and family members who made those months of lockdown bearable, many of whom also devoted time and care to reading various versions of the manuscript. I am immensely grateful to all of them.

My first reader and cheerleader was my sister, Dr. Judy Sprotzer, who demanded to see each chapter when it was done (or half done) and then shared her responses. The encouragement she provided, especially in the early days of writing, when I was asking myself whether to go on, was immeasurable. Constance Borde, Nancy Cott, Sandy Dijkstra, Sheila Malovany-Chevallier, Sonya Michel, Amy Schwartz, Michael Suleiman, Sherry Turkle, and Judith Wechsler read complete versions of the manuscript at various stages, and Christie McDonald, Daniel Suleiman, and Veronica Suleiman read individual chapters. All of their responses and suggestions proved invaluable as the manuscript moved toward its final form; even a casual remark could push me to rethink a whole chapter. My cousins Agnes Freund, Vivian Ziner-Cohen, and Shalom Gewurtz offered important information about family history; Hannah Cohen and Ezra Suleiman did the same for the history of the Suleiman family in Iraq. My grandchildren, Emma, Pablo, Alexander, and Nessa Suleiman, were and are a constant source of joy to me. This book is especially meant for them.

My editor at Stanford, Margo Irvin, has been truly a pleasure to work with, responding to all of my concerns and contributing important suggestions of her own. Her assistant Cindy Lim, as well as all the other staff at the press who have had a role in shepherding this book to publication, have my heartfelt thanks.

A few chapters were published, wholly or in part, in earlier versions. Parts of the Prologue first appeared as "The Silver Pin" in *Evocative Objects: Things We Think With*, ed. Sherry Turkle (Cambridge, MA: MIT Press, 2007). Chapter One's first incarnation appeared in *Harvard Review*, no. 24 (Spring 2003), and in Hungarian translation in *Szombat* 16, no. 8 (October 2004); a somewhat different version appeared in *On Being Adjacent to Historical Violence*, ed. Irene Kacandes (Berlin/Boston: De Gruyter, 2022). Parts of Chapter Two first appeared as "My War in Four Episodes" in *Agni* 33 (Spring 1991), reprinted subsequently in several anthologies and in my book *Risking Who One Is: Encounters with Contemporary Art and Literature* (Cambridge, MA: Harvard University Press, 1994). A slightly different version of Chapter Three appeared in *Tablet Magazine*, July 9, 2020, and was reprinted in *Nashim*, no. 39 (2021). In addition, readers of my previous memoir, *Budapest Diary: In Search of the Motherbook* (Lincoln: Nebraska University Press, 1996), may notice a few sprinklings of passages from that book in the early chapters, since I allowed myself those small bits of self-plagiarism.

The epigraphs to the book, in my translations, are from the following works: Georges Perec, *W ou le souvenir d'enfance* (Paris: Denoël, 1975); Irène Némirovsky, *Les chiens et les loups* (Paris: Albin Michel, 1940); Marcel Proust, *Le temps retrouvé* (*A la recherche du temps perdu*), Paris: NRF, 1927.

Photographs